ACADEMIC ADAPTATIONS

*Higher Education
Prepares for the 1980s
and 1990s*

PREPARED FOR THE CARNEGIE COUNCIL
ON POLICY STUDIES IN HIGHER EDUCATION

Verne A. Stadtman

ACADEMIC ADAPTATIONS

*Higher Education
Prepares for the 1980s
and 1990s*

 Jossey-Bass Publishers

San Francisco • Washington • London • 1980

ACADEMIC ADAPTATIONS
Higher Education Prepares for the 1980s and 1990s
Verne A. Stadtman

Copyright © by: The Carnegie Foundation
for the Advancement of Teaching

Jossey-Bass Inc., Publishers
433 California Street
San Francisco, California 94104

Jossey-Bass Limited
28 Banner Street
London EC1Y 8QE

*Copies are available from Jossey-Bass, San Francisco,
for the United States and Possessions, and for Canada,
Australia, New Zealand, and Japan.
Copies for the rest of the world are available
from Jossey-Bass, London.*

Library of Congress Cataloging in Publication Data

Stadtman, Verne A
  Academic adaptations.

  Bibliography: p. 204
  Includes index.
  1. Education, Higher—United States. I. Title.
LA227.3.S75   378.73   80-8000
ISBN 0-87589-480-1

Manufactured in the United States of America

JACKET DESIGN BY WILLI BAUM

FIRST EDITION   APR 27 1981

Code 8039

The Carnegie Council Series

The following publications are available from Jossey-Bass Inc., Publishers, 433 California Street, San Francisco, California 94104.

The Federal Role in Postsecondary
Education: Unfinished Business,
1975-1980
*The Carnegie Council on Policy
Studies in Higher Education*

More Than Survival: Prospects for
Higher Education in a Period
of Uncertainty
*The Carnegie Foundation for the
Advancement of Teaching*

Low or No Tuition: The Feasibility
of a National Policy for the
First Two Years of College
*The Carnegie Council on Policy
Studies in Higher Education*

Making Affirmative Action Work
in Higher Education: An Analysis
of Institutional and Federal
Policies with Recommendations
*The Carnegie Council on Policy
Studies in Higher Education*

The States and Higher Education:
A Proud Past and a Vital Future
*The Carnegie Foundation for the
Advancement of Teaching*

Presidents Confront Reality: From
Edifice Complex to University
Without Walls
*Lyman A. Glenny, John R. Shea,
Janet H. Ruyle, Kathryn H. Freschi*

Progress and Problems in Medical
and Dental Education: Federal
Support Versus Federal Control
*The Carnegie Council on Policy
Studies in Higher Education*

Managing Multicampus Systems:
Effective Administration in an
Unsteady State
Eugene C. Lee, Frank M. Bowen

Challenges Past, Challenges
Present: An Analysis of
American Higher Education
Since 1930
David D. Henry

Educational Leaves for Employees:
European Experience
for American Consideration
*Konrad von Moltke,
Norbert Schneevoigt*

Academic Adaptations: Higher
Education Prepares for the
1980s and 1990s
Verne A. Stadtman

The Carnegie Council on Policy
Studies in Higher Education:
A Summary of Reports and
Recommendations
*The Carnegie Council on Policy
Studies in Higher Education*

Three Thousand Futures:
The Next Twenty Years
for Higher Education
*The Carnegie Council on Policy
Studies in Higher Education*

*The following technical reports were published by the Carnegie Council on Policy
Studies in Higher Education.*

The States and Higher Education:
A Proud Past and a Vital Future
SUPPLEMENT to a Commentary of
The Carnegie Foundation for the
Advancement of Teaching
*The Carnegie Foundation for the
Advancement of Teaching*

Carnegie Council National
Surveys 1975-76: Faculty
Marginals (Vol. 2)
*The Carnegie Council on Policy
Studies in Higher Education*

A Classification of Institutions
of Higher Education: Revised
Edition
*The Carnegie Council on Policy
Studies in Higher Education*

Carnegie Council National
Surveys 1975-76: Undergraduate
Marginals (Vol. 3)
*The Carnegie Council on Policy
Studies in Higher Education*

Changing Practices in
Undergraduate Education
*Robert Blackburn, Ellen
Armstrong, Clifton Conrad,
James Didham, Thomas McKune*

Carnegie Council National
Surveys 1975-76: Graduate
Student Marginals (Vol. 4)
*The Carnegie Council on Policy
Studies in Higher Education*

Carnegie Council National
Surveys 1975-76: Aspects of
American Higher Education
(Vol. 1)
Martin Trow

Enrollment and Cost Effect of
Financial Aid Plans for Higher
Education
Joseph Hurd

Aspects of American
Higher Education, 1969-1975
Martin Trow

Market Conditions and Tenure for
Ph.D.'s in U.S. Higher Education:
Results from the 1975 Carnegie
Faculty Survey and Comparison
with Results from the 1973 ACE
Survey
Charlotte V. Kuh

Contents

Foreword

In 1968-69, with support from the Carnegie Commission on Higher Education, Harold Hodgkinson conducted studies of change in higher education during the previous decade. The basic data for his study were obtained from governmental sources, such as the U.S. Bureau of the Census and the National Center for Education Statistics; a questionnaire sent to college and universities presidents; and visits to campuses. His findings were published in 1971 under the title *Institutions in Transition*.

In *Academic Adaptations,* Verne Stadtman looks at American higher education approximately ten years later. He uses some of the same sources that were used by Dr. Hodgkinson to obtain his data and also relies heavily on questionnaires sent to presidents and other officers on the nation's campuses.

As one would expect, the years between the two studies have been marked by a continuation of some trends and by changes in others. Some important continuing trends have been the expansion of higher education resources throughout the country and the emergence of an egalitarian era that promises higher educational opportunities for everyone. One major change is that institutions that were anticipating continued growth in the 1960s were, by the end of the 1970s, contemplating the end of the era of expansion and expecting reduced enrollments and reduced levels of financial support. There are new kinds of students enrolling in colleges and universities as we begin the 1980s, and they have more to say about the kind of education they receive. Another change is that institutions that once sought out leaders who could manage expansion and plan for new missions are now seeking leaders who can husband limited resources and serve new "clienteles." Perhaps the most significant finding is that, when all is said and done, changes continue to occur. Higher education continues to be dynamic and adaptive.

As was the case with the study in 1969, this new one should be considered as viewing roughly one decade in the history of higher education as part of a continuum. The changes reported in this *Academic Adaptations* were made necessary, in part, by changes made in the past, and they will inevitably play a role in determining how colleges and universities develop in the future. Therefore, this report is simultaneously a recapitulation and a glimpse of future possibilities.

Verne A. Stadtman, Associate Director of the Carnegie Council, is well qualified to write this report on changes in institutions of higher education. As editor of the long series of reports and studies issued by the Council and its predecessor Carnegie Commission, he has had a unique opportunity to become immersed in research about and policy statements concerning higher education. He has met with leaders of higher education and visited colleges and universities in almost all of the fifty states. To this encyclopedic knowledge of the American system of higher education, he adds good judgment about it and deep insight into its workings. His report on *Academic Adaptations* will stand as the one best portrait of higher education in the United States entering the 1980s.

CLARK KERR
Chairman
The Carnegie Council on Policy
Studies in Higher Education

Preface

Although this study borrows heavily from the model provided by Harold Hodgkinson's *Institutions in Transition*, which was published in 1971, it is not intended to replicate his study in all respects. I also use statistics gathered from governmental sources, information gathered in site visits made by me and other members of the staff of the Carnegie Council on Policy Studies in Higher Education, and Carnegie Council survey data. But there are many ways in which this study differs from *Institutions in Transition*, and it is, in its final form, neither a point-by-point update of, nor a commentary on, Hodgkinson's work. It is simply another look at change in higher education—from a perspective of ten years later.

To obtain some of the information reported in *Academic Adaptations*, the Carnegie Council conducted three surveys of its own during summer and fall 1978. (See Appendix A for an abstract of the technical report for these surveys.) One survey was addressed to college and university presidents; another to student affairs officers; and a third to administrators concerned with financial or academic affairs. Although some of the questions Hodgkinson asked in his survey of 1968-69 were asked again in the Carnegie Council surveys, many were not. The Carnegie Council staff was concerned with somewhat different issues than he was, and with some of the same issues in greater depth than could be probed in 1968-69.

Some data sources that were available for this study did not exist in 1968-69. Hodgkinson's own recapitulation of basic data has been useful, but I have also used data that were not available to him. They include the surveys for the Carnegie Commission on Higher Education and the Carnegie Council, which gathered information from large samples of faculty members, graduate students, and undergraduates in 1969 and again in 1975 and 1976. Conducted under the direction of Martin Trow at the University of California, Berkeley, these surveys provide the most recent information available on some of the topics of concern here. Articles and books about institutional change are more abundant now than they were in 1969. *Presidents Confront Reality,* prepared under the sponsorship of the Carnegie Council by Lyman Glenny, John Shea, Janet Ruyle, and Kathryn H. Freschi, deserves special mention; it is a survey of institutional adaptations to declining enrollments and reduced resources in 1974.

Another work that was not available in 1969 is the *Classification of Institutions of Higher Education,* first issued by the Carnegie Commission on Higher Education in 1971 and then, in a revised edition, by the Carnegie Council on Policy Studies in Higher Education in 1976. Because this classification is used extensively in the chapters that follow, its basic structure should be familiar to readers at the start. Basically, the classification divides colleges and universities into six types: Doctorate-granting Institutions; Comprehensive Universities and Colleges; Liberal Arts Colleges; Two-Year Colleges and Institutes; Professional Schools and other Specialized Institutions; and Institutions of Nontraditional Study. These are further broken down in a rationale that gives attention to levels of research commitment, selectivity of admission policies, and comprehensiveness of the curriculum. In this study I am concerned almost exclusively with institutions in the first four categories, and a summary of subclassifications of these groups follows.

1. *Research Universities.* These are among the 100 leading institutions in federal funding for academic science and award at least 50 doctorates. *Research Universities I* includes the 50 leading universities in terms of federal support of academic science. *Research Universities II*

includes other institutions within the 100 leading institutions in federal funding and a few that do not meet these criteria but that have graduate programs of high quality and "impressive promise for future development." *Doctorate-granting Universities I* awarded 40 or more Ph.D.'s in 1973-74 or received at least $3 million in total federal support in either 1973-74 or 1974-75. *Doctorate-granting Universities II* awarded at least 20 Ph.D.'s in 1973-74 (or 10 in certain selected fields).

2. *Comprehensive Universities and Colleges.* These are institutions offering a liberal arts program in addition to professional or occupational programs. Many offer the master's degree, but have no or very limited doctorate programs. *Comprehensive Universities and Colleges I* had at least two professional or occupational programs and enrolled at least 2,000 students. *Comprehensive Universities and Colleges II* offered at least one professional or occupational program. Private institutions with less than 1,500 students and public institutions with less than 1,000 students were not included in this category even if they offered programs other than in the liberal arts, because they were not considered sufficiently comprehensive.

3. *Liberal Arts Colleges. Liberal Arts Colleges I* are highly selective four-year colleges offering a liberal arts program. *Liberal Arts Colleges II* are all other four-year liberal arts colleges.

4. *Two-Year Colleges and Institutes.* These classifications are described in greater detail in the introduction to the full classification report (Carnegie Council, 1976, pp. iv-xii).

Some of the information reported in this study comes from site visits made by members of the Carnegie Council staff to 26 colleges and universities in early spring 1979.

Finally, I should point out that this study was planned from the beginning as a companion to the final report of the Carnegie Council on Policy Studies in Higher Education, *Three Thousand Futures: The Next Twenty Years for Higher Education* (1980). One result of that relationship is that some of the subjects that might have been discussed here in considerable detail had they not already been extensively addressed by the Council's final report are only touched upon lightly so that unnecessary duplication can be avoided. I have not, however, avoided mentioning information and trends that are discussed in the Council's final report where readers are likely to need them in order to follow the discussion and conclusions I offer here. The relationship between this study and the final report of the Council should in no way be interpreted, however, to mean that *Academic Adaptations* expresses the views of the Council or carries official endorsement by either the Council or any of its individual members.

Acknowledgments

This study has benefited from the contributions and assistance of many people. I am indebted to Arthur Levine and John Shea for their assistance in developing the surveys of 1978 and for conducting most of the site visits; to C. E. Christian for help in the site visits and for providing some of the statistical information found in Chapter 5; to Sura Johnson, who coordinated the surveys with skill and enormous care; to Sandra Elman, who participated in the field visits and served ably as research assistant for the project; to Anne Machung, who provided valuable research assistance in the concluding months of the study; to Nancy A. Blumenstock, who not only edited this manuscript but assumed other editorial responsibilities so that I could give this study more of my time; and to Claudia White, who so quietly and efficiently coordinated preparation of this manuscript and attended to countless other details associated with the project. Finally, I want to thank Clark Kerr, not only for this assignment, but also for the opportunity to join him in what has been a stimulating, enlightening, and significant enterprise.

Washington, D.C.   Verne A. Stadtman
September 1980

The Author

Verne A. Stadtman is vice-president of the Carnegie Foundation for the Advancement of Teaching. At the time this book was written, he was associate director and editor of the Carnegie Council on Policy Studies in Higher Education. Stadtman has also served in similar capacities at the Carnegie Commission on Higher Education. For the the Council and Commission he assumed staff responsibility for reports on black colleges, instructional technology, education in the noncollegiate sector, and the undergraduate curriculum.

Stadtman is author of *The University of California 1868-1968*, a centennial history of California's statewide university, and is co-editor, with David Riesman, of *Academic Transformation—Seventeen Institutions Under Pressure.*

ACADEMIC ADAPTATIONS

*Higher Education
Prepares for the 1980s
and 1990s*

PREPARED FOR THE CARNEGIE COUNCIL
ON POLICY STUDIES IN HIGHER EDUCATION

1

Happenings on the Way
to the 1980s

Nothing survives the passing of years without change, and, just as very hard rocks yield their shape and size to nature's elements, colleges and universities, however steeped they may be in tradition, also change to accommodate forces of history and social developments. It makes sense, therefore, to take stock occasionally and find out how colleges and universities are different now than they were the last time we looked at them systematically. By doing so, we may be able to anticipate the shape of higher education in the years ahead. At the very least, we may learn something about the changes students, faculty members, and administrators must take into consideration as they plan their futures.

Higher Education in 1969

The characterizing feature of American higher education in 1969 was the crescendo of student activism, dissent, and disruption that had started early in the 1960s and at the end of that decade approached the peak of its volume and intensity. Martin Luther King, Jr., was murdered in 1968, and, across the country, in their shock, guilt, and indignation, students protested and demonstrated on behalf of efforts to improve the lot of black students on college campuses. The war in Vietnam, the presence of military training programs on campuses, university involvement in defense-related research, and a rash of maverick political, social, and campus issues troubled students and brought them into conflict with campus and civil authorities (Riesman and Stadtman, 1973). By the end of 1969, the fatalities at Kent State and Jackson State that climaxed this era of student unrest were only five months away.

On many campuses political action was interpreted as evidence of student dissatisfaction with educational programs and institutional governance. Students began to talk about these things themselves, and colleges and universities began to look seriously at curricular adjustments and alternatives and to expand the role of students in campus decision making.

But the resulting reform was more than a sop to student power. It was also an accommodation to a greater diversity of students than colleges had known before. Open doors that made colleges and universities more hospitable to members of minority races and to young people who had been educationally disadvantaged in their pre-college years brought not only more students but more exceptions to campus standards and regulations. Differences among students became important, and programs designed for homogeneous student bodies had to be adjusted. Openness to new kinds of students, therefore, engendered receptiveness to new instructional technologies and curricular change.

Some of the programmatic reforms of American colleges and universities in 1969 were designed to save money or generate income. David Henry, a university president at that time, explained that financial difficulties began to appear in 1968. Except for a relatively few institutions that remained small throughout the 1950s and 1960s as a matter of policy, colleges and universities had been growing rapidly since the end of World War II. By 1969 the whole higher education enterprise was not only bigger, it was also more costly. And money became harder to get. More specifically, Henry (1975, p. 135) said:

> The unexpected acceleration in the general inflation rate magnified costs, and dollars bought less. Federal resources that had gone to institutional income declined as a proportion of educational expenditures; unsettled economic conditions affected income from

endowment and gifts; and tuition income could not be significantly increased without diminishing returns or incurring political opposition or both. What increases there were in public appropriations were often earmarked for community colleges or programs in the health sciences, including medicine. Capital expenditures followed the same course.

Hodgkinson (1971, p. 24) found that funding was the number one concern of virtually all college presidents in 1968-69. For college presidents today who are inclined to say, "It was ever thus," it should be pointed out that for many presidents in 1968-69 the experience of hard times was new.

Second to funding, the problem of most concern to college presidents was growth. "Almost every questionnaire mentioned the word—more students, more faculty, more facilities" (Hodgkinson, 1971, p. 25). How quaint that notion seems in 1979! But it was not based on wishful thinking. The first report of the Carnegie Commission on Higher Education came out in December 1968 and explained the matter this way: "Today's enrollment is almost 6 million students on a full-time equivalent (FTE) basis. More than one-half of this growth took place in the decade from 1958 to 1967. Estimates indicate that enrollment will pass 8 million by 1976, and this figure may well rise to 9 million if Carnegie Commission or other proposals are adopted to remove financial barriers for students from low-income families" (p. 3). The Commission's estimate was a little optimistic but close to the mark (actual enrollment in 1976 was 7.8 million). Of more significance is the fact that it was consistent with the general expectations of the time.

That the end of the Vietnam war would result in decreased enrollment by males who found going to college an honorable alternative to involuntary military service was not anticipated, and the public perception that college attendance was not the reliable kind of insurance against unemployment or underemployment it had historically been had not yet dawned. To the extent anyone knew about them, low birthrates in the 1960s, which would result in fewer college students in the

1980s, were a matter for interesting speculation. *Growth was the present reality,* and presidents were accountable to their trustees, their faculties and students, their state governments, their alumni, and the public for how they led their institutions' adjustments to it.

The growth in the 1960s was accommodated by extensive college building and expansion. Colleges and universities spent $21.5 billion for buildings and improvements during the decade (National Center for Education Statistics [NCES], *Financial Statistics,* appropriate issues). The National Center for Education Statistics (1978a, p. xlii) reports that 702 new institutions were established between 1960 and 1969. Of these, 534 (3 out of 4) were public institutions. That statistic says a great deal about the economic condition of state governments in the 1960s. Some of them had built up considerable reserves during World War II; they also participated in the general prosperity of the country. They had the fiscal capacity needed to expand higher education. More importantly, such expansion seemed to be supported by the general public.

Part of the public confidence derived from the widely presumed success of colleges and universities in their roles as cultivators of higher culture and trainers of manpower and leadership for the productive pursuits of the nation. It also derived from the respect of the public for the nation's scientific achievements during and after World War II. These achievements were closely linked to the intellectual and physical resources devoted to science at American universities.

The universities' role in the scientific achievements of the nation generated more than public support. It also contributed to the maturation of what Jencks and Riesman called *The Academic Revolution* (1968). Fundamentally, this revolution involved the gradual assumption of more authority on university and college campuses by members of the academic profession. For most practical purposes, the faculty already had control of the methods of instruction; the curriculum; admission of students; and the hiring, retention, and promotion of their colleagues. Now they set the standards for student performance and also for the award of the Ph.D., and thus for access to their own profession. College and university presidents normally begin their careers in the academic ranks and, increasingly, are appointed to their jobs with the explicit approval of the faculty they are selected to lead. Through their academic disciplines and their professional and scholarly associations, the faculty maintain standards for academic research. Independently, they choose their own research projects and cultivate outside sources of support. The public's support of scientific activities after the war tended to increase the authority and independence of faculty members and contributed to the success of the academic revolution, which may have peaked in 1969.

To summarize, then, the major contextual factors that affected higher education when Hodgkinson studied it for his work *Institutions in Transition* (1971) were campus dissent and disruption related to both social and campus issues; an opening of the campuses to different types of students than had been admitted before; accommodations to individual differences among students through innovations in programs and instructional technologies; greater concern for the rising costs of operating increasingly expensive institutions; anticipation of continued enrollment growth for the ensuing decade; reasonably strong public confidence in higher education; and the acceptance of extensive authority in college and university affairs by the academic profession.

The Intervening Years

In comparing the contexts in which colleges and universities operated in 1969 with those that prevail in 1979, one gets the impression that old problems are never really solved—they just get renamed and redefined. One reason for this impression is that, although colleges and universities tend to follow the leader in their responses to challenges and opportunities, they do not do so in concert, except perhaps as members of consortia or multicampus systems. Each approaches problems in its own way and on its own schedule. Some institutions solve a problem; others accommodate it; still others founder on it. The result is that the problems that confront all institutions of higher education are in evidence for a long time. They linger in some places long after others have responded to them successfully. Eventually, solved or not, they simply change form.

A good example of this phenomenon is provided by the fiscal concerns of colleges and universities. As we have seen, in 1969 the problems usually were defined in terms of the increased costs of operating expanded institutions and systems just when inflation was depreciating available revenues. In the 1970s, matters got worse as inflation continued, but the country experienced a recession as well. Then, in 1976 the financial prospects of colleges and universities began to look brighter as the recession ended. Some state treasuries were again accumulating reserves, but, before the outlook for more state support could really brighten, a taxpayers' revolt, first in California, but soon in other states, forced governments to reduce spending and turned the "bright" switch for college and university funding prospects to "dim." By 1978, then, "financing" was still the number one problem of leaders of higher education. In the Carnegie Council's surveys of that year, about one-third of the presidents of public colleges and universities and more than one-half of the presidents of private institutions give financial problems that ranking. The public's frugal mood has obvious consequences for all institutions. For public colleges and universities, appropriations are smaller, and fewer new projects are funded. Private colleges that hoped for new state support see such prospects growing more remote.

Another dimension of the financial difficulties of some colleges and universities involves a loss of revenue from tuition and other student fees as enrollments decline. Thus, financing problems overlapped a second-ranked concern that will be increasingly prominent in the 1980s.

The concern for growth that characterized higher education in 1969 is now converted into a concern for excess capacity. A few institutions that resisted growth or were unable to accommodate it in the 1960s and 1970s approach the 1980s without the burden of large investments in buildings and equipment to amortize and without commitments to faculty members for whom there are no students. But even these few institutions may face difficulties in the 1980s if they have to compete for students with lower-priced, program-rich, neighboring institutions.

The irony is that enrollments have, in fact, grown. Between 1970 and 1978, enrollments increased by 2.7 million FTE students—an increase of 46 percent. The increase alone is greater than the total higher education enrollment in most other countries of the world. But it does not represent an unlimited market for educational services. Often overlooked by college planners is the fact that the increase is divided among 3,100 institutions, many of which were not built or not operating at full capacity in 1969. Moreover, the large numbers hide the fact that substantial numbers of students are now more than 22 years old and attend classes only part-time; many students now alternate college attendance with periods of a term or more devoted to work, travel, or leisure; and many students now do not complete their work toward a degree after they enroll. To add to the problem, the rate of enrollment growth has already been slowed down by such factors as the termination of compulsory military service for young men who are not enrolled in college and the widely accepted belief that a college education is no longer a guarantee of desirable employment.

The relationship of education to work careers was underscored in the 1970s by Sidney Marland who, as U.S. Commissioner of Education, became a strong and articulate advocate of career education. Some of the impact of this movement was rhetorical because higher education has always been utilized in preparing for careers, even when it was not highly specialized. The historical significance of the career education movement of the 1970s is that it tended to legitimate and even elevate the status of educational programs that concentrated on skills needed in specific occupations. By suggesting that such programs were not only appropriate but desirable in institutions of higher learning, the movement encouraged institutions to expand their offerings and acquire the physical capabilities that made it possible for them to attract different kinds of students than they had reached in the past.

The consequences of these efforts to seek out new types of students are now quite clear:

1. Students have been diverted from liberal arts programs into vocational, preprofessional, and professional programs. In 1977 the Carnegie Foundation for the Advancement of Teaching reported that the percentage of undergraduates majoring in the "professions" (a category that includes vocational and occupational programs) increased from 38 to 58 between 1969 and 1976. During the same period, the percentage of undergraduate majors fell from 9 to 5 in the humanities; from 18 to 12 in the social sciences; and from 12 to 11 in the sciences (Carnegie Foundation, 1977, p. 103).

2. Many liberal arts colleges have added one or more professional departments or schools to their programs. The most frequent new additions are in business, but new programs in engineering, nursing, and other health-related fields are also common. At these institutions, education programs have shrunk because of the decreasing job market for teachers. The net result, however, seems to be that more and more liberal arts colleges are becoming comprehensive institutions.

3. The distinction between specialized vocational and technical schools and the occupationally oriented programs of more "academic" institutions is becoming blurred.

4. Some colleges are under pressure to offer higher-level degrees (typically the master's) for short-term, specialized programs in occupational fields than those offered for four years of liberal arts education.

5. Colleges across the country are experimenting with new curricula, new calendars, and new instructional technologies in attempts to match the learning needs of the new types of students. The 1970s has been a decade of innovation, partly to improve learning for all students and partly to serve new clienteles better.

6. The faculty requirements for the new programs differ considerably from those of offerings for full-time students in traditional courses. Part-time instructors are often preferred, and they are likely to be drawn from the pool of available practitioners employed by business and industry in the nearby community rather than from college and university graduate schools. Unfortunately, this further erodes the already diminished job opportunities for new Ph.D.'s looking for teaching positions in colleges and universities.

The extent to which faculty, generally, influence the course of higher education in the coming decades may be determined by the successes or failures of faculty unionism. In 1969, the faculty of the City University of New York chose a bargaining agent and, by so doing, brought national attention to efforts to unionize the academic profession. These efforts initially were most successful in public community colleges but gradually spread to other public institutions in which faculty members felt left out of institutional decision making— even when the decisions that were made affected their working conditions and livelihood. By 1976 faculty members had unionized about 430 colleges and universities (Garbarino, 1977, p. 30). Wherever it exists, collective bargaining introduces a new element into the governance procedures of colleges.

In some cases faculty unionism increases the likelihood of the involvement of state government in institutional affairs. Wherever collective bargaining has forced final decisions to levels beyond the institution itself, it strengthens a tendency in that direction that has been apparent since the 1960s. For many public colleges and universities, the locus of ultimate governing authority has shifted from the trustees and administrators of individual institutions to statewide coordinating agencies. Regulations at both the state and federal level accompany public funding for institutions. College and university presidents and their key administrative associates find that a great deal of time is spent adjusting institutional policies to the demands of government agencies. Administrative skills become more important than intellectual leadership and educational statesmanship. The burden of governmental reporting and compliance is felt by public and private institutions alike and has vastly increased in the 1970s with the expansion of student aid programs, the enforcement of affirmative action policies that govern student admissions and staff hiring, and regulations that impose minimum health and safety standards on institutions.

Although the authority of university and college presidents is eroded to some extent by these governmental intrusions, it may be stronger internally. One reason is that the president and his fellow administrators are, in fact, the principal interpreters and enforcers of all of the new governmental regulations and controls at the institutional level. Another is that, in times of fiscal stringency, the interests of all units in an institution are best served by centralized, rather than diffused, authority. Few presidents can survive periods such as those that higher education has been going through in the past decade without the authority to plan, coordinate, consolidate, and eliminate programs, and to divert funds to the departments and divisions that most need them. By and large, the governing boards of American colleges and universities have given presidents that authority and supported them when they exercised it.

After the student protests of the 1960s, many observers expected students to play a larger role in institutional governance than they had in the past. At least nominally, students now do have formal representation on important administrative and academic committees on many campuses. On a few campuses that were visited by members of the Carnegie Council staff, students were regarded as at least equal in power to the faculty. But my impression is that most of this power is exercised by students informally as consumers of education, rather than as part of the formal machinery of institutional governance.

Shifts of power and authority, changed levels and sources of funding, reduced enrollments, efforts to reach new clienteles, pressures to expand career education (often at the expense of liberal arts), shortages of jobs for new Ph.D.'s, the continued growth of collective bargaining, and the increasing influence of state and federal governments—all of these changes occurred within higher education in the 1970s.

External Developments

Colleges and universities are never isolated from the major events and trends of the times in which they exist, and many of their internal changes are responses to the swirl of the world around them. Five events in the 1970s should be highlighted because they significantly altered the context in which colleges and universities operate.

1. The 26th Amendment to the Constitution, ratified in 1971, lowered the voting age and made 98 percent of the national college student body eligible to vote. As a special interest electorate, students are not as yet fully organized, although there are efforts to enlist their votes on education-related issues and lobbies claiming to represent their views in state and national capitals. Organized or not, however, students can no longer be ignored as interested parties in the development of public as well as campus educational policy.

2. The arrest of five men who broke into the offices of the Democratic National headquarters in the Watergate complex in Washington, D.C., in 1972 touched off a series of political scandals that reached the highest offices of the land and resulted in the resignation of Richard M. Nixon from the presidency in 1974.

   Watergate raised questions about the integrity of all social institutions and inspired government officials and agencies to become increasingly sensitive to criticism, more protective of their credibility, and more insistent upon the accountability of all who benefit from their support. At another level, Watergate made the general public less confident of the morality of its leaders, and this concern translated into increased interest in the capabilities of colleges and universities (from which leadership is presumed to come) to provide ethical and moral education.

Part of the recent and continuing effort to strengthen general education and liberal learning in the college curriculum responds to this concern.

3.   One feature of American compulsory military service, which ended in 1973, was that exemptions were extended to college students. When the draft ended, the artificial demand for higher learning created by exemption ceased. The termination of the draft explains a significant portion of the decrease in enrollments, particularly as it is evident among white males, in the 1970s. Another effect of the end of the draft is that campus-centered dissent from unpopular national military and foreign policies has abated.

4.   The most serious depression to hit the country since World War II occurred in 1974-75. Coupled with continuing inflation, it posed severe problems for institutions forced to pay larger bills with smaller revenues. Increased fuel costs in 1975 were particularly burdensome to colleges and universities in regions with cold winters. The costs of attending college were beyond the reach of many young people, and student enrollments in private institutions dropped noticeably during these years. During the depression, unemployment reached 9.2 percent, and stories about Ph.D.'s driving taxis and college graduates washing dishes or working on assembly lines were told and retold in college dormitories, dining commons, and placement centers. These challenges to long-standing beliefs about the economic returns of education, popularized by books like *Education and Jobs: The Great Training Robbery* (Berg, 1970) and *The Case Against College* (Bird, 1975), cast public doubt on presumptions of an inevitable link between success and the college degree. Many colleges attempted to restore the faith by strengthening programs that offered occupational and professional training, and the strength of the liberal arts in college curricula was eroded somewhat as a consequence. It was widely expected that increasingly gloomy employment prospects for graduates would keep thousands of young people out of college entirely.

5. The federal government, for most of the post-World War II era, was a strong partner of American universities in the development and support of scientific research. But the federal government's share of support of research activities in colleges and universities began to decline after 1966, when it reached 73.6 percent of the total until 1977, when it was 67 percent (Carnegie Council, 1980, Supplement J). Although the nation's 133 doctorate-granting institutions were most directly affected by these reductions, all colleges ultimately felt the consequences in the form of a slowdown in knowledge production and the curtailment of opportunities to apprentice prospective college teachers in major research activities in academic settings.

The realities and consequences of all these trends—internal and external to campus—have affected different types of institutions in different ways. The record of their adaptations to the forces at work on the events of the 1980s is the burden of the chapters that follow.

Part One

People in Higher Education

This part is concerned with college and university students, faculty members, trustees, and presidents—the people who are directly involved in American higher education. Their numbers, interests, and needs affect the character and extensiveness of the programs colleges and universities offer; their skills determine the level and quality of instruction; and their satisfaction with campus conditions and with the results of educational efforts contribute to the stability of their institutions. Any adequate understanding of the changes that are taking place in higher education begins, therefore, with an awareness of some important changes in the groups of people who most prominently take part in it.

2

Students

Students provide the ultimate rationale for almost every change that occurs in American higher education. If colleges and universities want to get bigger or if planners believe higher education institutions should become more numerous, their cases often rest on proof that there are more students to accommodate. If governmental agencies wish to reduce public financial support of higher education, they quickly try to establish that fewer students will want to enroll. Departments that want to add new programs of instruction often make their case on the basis that many students who want such programs can't get them, that students who fail to get them will be handicapped in their postgraduate pursuits, or that the new programs will attract new types of students to the college. Changes in schedules, in the level of difficulty, or in the specific location of instruction may be justified in terms of both real and perceived changes in the characteristics of learners. Even the research activities of universities are often defended on grounds that the faculty members who engage in them are in a better position than those who do not to enrich the teaching they provide for their students.

The astonishing growth in the capacity of institutions of higher education in the 1960s and 1970s was rationalized almost entirely on the basis of anticipated increases in the numbers of students seeking admission. And the students came. By fall 1979, 11 million (headcount) of them were enrolled. This is more than one-third more than the 8 million enrolled

in 1969, and about two and one-third times more than the
4.8 million enrolled in 1963.[1]

Part of this enrollment growth is caused by an increase
in the birthrate after World War II. Babies born at that time
attained college age in the 1950s and 1960s, strained the
capacities of existing institutions, and caused new ones to
be built.

But higher birthrates are only one of the reasons for
enrollment growth. During the 1960s there was also concern,
in and out of the colleges, for the fact that the student bodies
of institutions of higher learning were dominated by young,
white males who came from the privileged socioeconomic
sector of our society. America's concerns for social justice and
for extending the educational attainment of its populace fueled
a movement to encourage colleges to open their doors to
previously excluded groups and to take affirmative action on
behalf of more equal treatment of women and members of
racial minorities. Admissions and recruiting officers made
concerted efforts to find qualified members of minority groups
to enroll—and sometimes bent the rules to get them in. Colleges
strengthened their efforts to help students with inadequate
learning skills catch up with their classmates and stay in school.
Financial aid programs for students helped to lower economic
barriers to college attendance.

As a result of such efforts, the number of black students
enrolled in colleges and universities doubled—from 492,000 in
1969 to 1.1 million in 1977 (U.S. Bureau of the Census, 1970,
1979). The enrollment trends for members of other minority
groups are not as clear. Statistics on groups other than blacks
and whites were not disaggregated by the U.S. Bureau of the
Census in 1969, but deducting blacks from a category called
"negro and other races" left 115,000 that year (U.S. Bureau
of the Census, 1970, p. 9). More recently (1979), the U.S.
Bureau of the Census reported that in 1977 there were 418,000

---

[1]Full-time equivalent (FTE) enrollment was 3.7 million (estimated) in 1963, 6.7
million (estimated) in 1969, and 8.3 million in 1976 (NCES, 1978d, p. 26).

students of Spanish origin and 190,000 of Mexican origin in American colleges. Some of that enrollment (though we cannot guess how much) undoubtedly was a net gain over enrollments for these groups 10 years earlier.

Until the women's movement gathered momentum in the 1960s and 1970s, the idea that women could combine education, careers, and parenting was not widely accepted. But, as the professions and other attractive occupational fields began to open up to women with the appropriate preparation, colleges began to play a stronger role in helping them to broaden their opportunities. They did so by helping women obtain financial assistance; working to break down old prejudices that lurked in the dark corners of some academic departments; providing more flexible class schedules to accommodate mothers and working women; and, on some campuses, providing child-care centers. There is no dearth of women who are academically qualified to be admitted to college; thus, intense recruiting efforts directed at women occur mainly at competing women's colleges or at formerly all-male institutions that are now co-educational. Even in the absence of strong recruiting efforts, however, the enrollment of women increased from about 3 million in 1969 to 4.8 million in 1977 (U.S. Bureau of the Census, 1970, 1979). By October 1979, for the first time in the history of American higher education, women constituted a majority (50.7 percent) of college enrollments in the United States (Magarell, 1979, p. 6).

The increased college attendance of older women pursuing a delayed or interrupted education is particularly impressive. In 1972, there were 418,000 women more than 35 years old enrolled in American colleges and universities; by 1976, there were 700,000 (NCES, 1978a). In my visits to colleges and universities in spring 1978, I met a surprising number of women who had received bachelor's degrees, had gone to work at female-stereotyped jobs, had found them stultifying, and had then returned to college to learn things that they really cared about and that might prepare them for interesting careers— including positions on college faculties.

At Hunter College a member of our staff was told about a growing senior citizen population. For the most part, these women come to get degrees. They are described as a "great bunch," highly curious, and good students. Some of them are well-off and come to class "with their furs and their dangling jewelry. They have great respect for their teachers and seem to get along well with the younger students. They keep telling the younger students who don't want to work hard how important a college education is." But not all of the older students on the nation's campuses are women, and interactions between older and younger students are no longer unusual. Older students now include men who are resuming college studies to enhance their chances for career advancement or to retrain for new careers. They also include men and women who have reached retirement age and attend college as a constructive and stimulating way to use their leisure time. Between 1972 and 1976, the enrollment of students over 25 increased from one-fourth of the total to about one-third (NCES, 1978d). And the story continues to unfold. In 1978 more than three-fourths (78 percent) of the college presidents in the country report that, in the first five years of the 1980s, they expect to emphasize recruitment of students in the older age groups (Carnegie Council Surveys, 1978).

The stage for this kind of emphasis was set in the 1960s and 1970s as colleges began to respond more sympathetically than in the past to the needs of students who could not attend classes full-time. For many years, at night or on weekends, campus parking lots were full, and lights burned, only on the campuses of two-year community colleges. The phenomenon is more general now. The techniques for attracting students at unconventional times are numerous: offering the same courses at different times of the day or week; offering instruction at off-campus locations; or making arrangements for independent study (for a more detailed description of these options, see Carnegie Council on Policy Studies in Higher Education, 1980, Supplement G). The increased convenience of split-level schedules and off-campus learning sites contributed to an increase in the proportion of students who work at least 50 percent time from 30 percent of all undergraduates in 1969 to 54 percent in 1976 (Carnegie Surveys, 1969-70, 1975-76).

The increased flexibility of college attendance patterns became a hallmark of higher education in the 1970s, and one of its most radical forms was made possible by the legitimization of the "stopout" as a means of breaking up the traditional gestation period of the wisdom and learning perceived to be embodied in a degree. Students were encouraged, for the first time, to stop out of college for a semester or more before receiving their degrees or otherwise terminating their college attendance. The time was to be spent working, traveling, visiting other institutions, or engaging in some other constructive activity. In 1969, 17 percent of the undergraduates in American colleges and universities had stopped out; in 1976, the proportion had reached 26 percent (Carnegie Surveys, 1969-70, and 1975-76).

Student Ability

When the Carnegie Council asked college presidents about the quality of students in 1978 as compared to 1970, the response was as follows:

Quality enhanced	40.3%
Quality both enhanced and impaired	32.7
Quality impaired	9.6
No change	14.7
Don't know	2.7

Presidents explain the quality was up because in 1978 there were more candidates for admission to choose from and because the students they enrolled were better prepared than students in 1970. Presidents of the more selective institutions were particularly likely to see their students in those terms. If grades can be taken at face value, this view is amply supported by records of high school achievement compiled by entering freshmen. In fall 1978, 26 percent of all entering freshmen in American colleges and universities had grades of

B, and 44 percent had grades of B+ or better. In 1969, 24 percent had grades of B and only 22 percent had grades of B+ or better (Table 1). But the grade inflation that has been experienced in the colleges in recent years has also found its way into secondary schools. And the fact that there are large numbers of candidates for admission has another side that is frequently mentioned by the presidents of less-selective institutions: Some of the entering students lack the basic skills to succeed academically. In fact, 91 percent of the presidents who say that the quality of their students has been impaired cite lack of skills as a reason.

Table 1. Average high school grades of entering
freshmen, 1969, 1978

	All institutions 1969	All institutions 1978	All universities 1978	All four-year colleges, 1978	All two-year colleges, 1978
A or A+	4%	11%	18%	11%	5%
A—	2	13	19	15	7
B+	16	20	23	22	17
B	24	26	22	26	30
B—	16	13	9	12	16
C+	12	11	6	9	15
C	15	7	3	5	11
D	1	0.3	0.1	0.2	1

Source: Creager and others, 1969; Astin, King, and Richardson, 1978.

The evidence supporting concerns for a decline in student quality is impressive and, by now, familiar to everyone who has been following recent discussions of standardized testing. Between 1969-70 and 1977-78, the average scores of high school seniors taking the College Board's Scholastic Aptitude Test declined from 460 to 429 on the verbal portion and from 488 to 468 on the mathematical portion. The National Assessment of Educational Progress also reported a decline in the reading comprehension and writing abilities of American 17-year-olds (Levine, 1978, pp. 58-59).[2] To make up for student deficiencies, 85 percent of American colleges and universities now offer

[2]See also discussions of student ability in Carnegie Council on Policy Studies in Higher Education (1980).

compensatory or remedial education programs, and the presidents of 75 percent say that such programs are more important
now than they were in 1969-70.

The Trend Toward Seriousness

When asked to describe how students at their institutions were
different in 1978 than they were in 1969-70, 24 percent of the
college presidents responding to the Carnegie Council Surveys
of 1978 say students are "serious about their studies," and
another 14 percent characterize them simply as "more serious."

In Table 2 some of the reasons entering freshmen considered very important in deciding to go to college in 1978
are listed. "Learning more about things" and "Gaining a general
education" both rate high on this list, and only in two-year
colleges does the objective of gaining a general education rank
as important to less than 70 percent of the freshmen.

Table 2. Reasons cited by entering freshmen in 1978 as "very important"
in their decision to go to college
(percentage of freshmen by institutional type)

	All institutions	All universities	All four-year colleges	All two-year colleges
Get a better job	75%	74%	73%	79%
Learn more about things	74	76	75	71
Gain a general education	68	71	71	63
Make more money	60	59	57	65
Meet new and interesting people	57	63	59	50
Prepare for graduate school	44	50	46	39
Improve reading-study skills	38	35	41	36
Become a more cultured person	34	36	37	30
Parents wanted me to go	29	27	30	28
Get away from home	8	10	8	6
Could not find a job	4	3	4	6
Nothing better to do	2	2	2	2

Source: Astin, King, and Richardson, 1978.

The top-ranked objective of students, however, is to "get a better job," and it is cited as important by a least 73 percent of the students at all institutions. The priority thus assigned to careers may not really be new and may only indicate greater candor in the matter. But it is widespread. Only in two-year colleges, where a career orientation has been strong for years, do fewer than 75 percent of the deans of student affairs say that student interest in careers has increased since 1969-70 (Table 3). In 1978, 42 percent of the college presidents also cite career orientation as a characteristic of students that has become more obvious since 1969-70 (Carnegie Council Surveys, 1978).

One way undergraduates demonstrate their career interests is by their choices of majors. As reported by The Carnegie Foundation for the Advancement of Teaching (1977), enrollment in majors with a professional or occupational orientation increased substantially between 1969 and 1976, while enrollment in the humanities, social sciences, and physical sciences all decreased (Figure 1).

Another student characteristic that may be related to the undergraduate's concerns for careers is the extent to which students are "more self-oriented." This assessment is made by 13 percent of the college presidents and is shared by 90 percent of the student affairs officers at Research Universities I, by 85 percent of the student affairs officers at Liberal Arts Colleges I, and by no less than 70 percent of such officers at all other institutions (Table 3). Levine (forthcoming) considers this characteristic of students so important that he makes it a major theme in his detailed study of students in the 1970s.

Lifestyles

Students have become more independent in many ways. As we have seen, more of them are now beyond the traditional age for college attendance; some even have children of their own. Student financial aid has diminished the dependence of students on their families and makes them less obligated to observe the lifestyle preferences of their parents. And they are no longer innocent: The culture that surrounds them is explicit on many

Table 3. Proportions of students in 1977-78 with selected characteristics, by percentages, as rated by student affairs officers, by Carnegie classification

	Research Universities		Doctorate-granting Institutions		Comprehensive Colleges and Universities		Liberal Arts Colleges		Two-Year Colleges
	I	II	I	II	I	II	I	II	
Proportion who are:									
Career-oriented									
Majority	94%	98%	91%	93%	88%	91%	75%	77%	82%
Some	6	2	10	7	12	9	25	23	18
Compared to students in 1969-70 the proportion has:									
Increased	77	84	76	85	75	77	87	76	60
Remained the same	23	9	24	9	25	21	13	17	35
Decreased	0	6	0	6	0	2	0	7	5
Concerned with self									
Majority	90	83	84	79	76	73	85	71	71
Some	10	14	16	21	23	27	15	29	27
Compared to students in 1969-70 the proportion has:									
Increased	58	59	52	49	48	52	41	43	39
Remained the same	43	29	48	45	50	46	59	52	60
Decreased	0	13	0	6	2	2	0	5	1

Concerned with material success									
Majority	82	79	66	79	78	68	64	58	59
Some	18	19	33	21	21	29	34	40	37
Compared to students in 1969-70 the proportion has:									
Increased	66	81	68	70	63	56	72	46	48
Remained the same	34	16	29	24	37	41	28	52	50
Decreased	0	3	2	6	1	3	0	2	3
Practical									
Majority	49	81	71	74	59	49	53	58	53
Some	51	19	27	26	41	51	47	37	47
Compared to students in 1969-70 the proportion has:									
Increased	54	63	64	64	49	39	48	46	30
Remained the same	46	34	36	36	51	58	50	47	68
Decreased	0	3	0	0	1	3	2	7	2

Note: Student affairs officers were asked to consider 21 adjectival phrases describing undergraduates and indicate whether the characteristic applied to the majority, some, or very few of the students on their campuses. This table presents responses on four of the characteristics listed. Others included: concerned with campus issues, concerned with international issues, change-oriented, idealistic, pessimist, well-groomed. For a more thorough discussion of responses, see Levine, forthcoming.
Source: Carnegie Council Surveys, 1978.

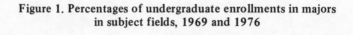

Figure 1. Percentages of undergraduate enrollments in majors
in subject fields, 1969 and 1976

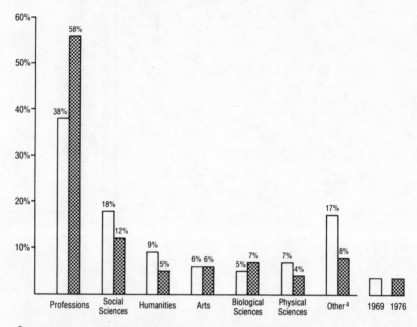

[a]Includes "no major" and such subjects as ethnic studies, women's studies, and en-
vironmental studies, all of which have very low enrollments.
Note: An earlier version of this figure appeared in The Carnegie Foundation for the
Advancement of Teaching (1977), in which there was a miscalculation of majors
in the social sciences and physical sciences. This is corrected in the figure above.
Numbers may not add to 100 owing to rounding.
Source: Carnegie Council Surveys, 1969-70, 1975-76.

subjects that were seldom discussed publicly by earlier generations, and their senses are continuously treated to the sights
and sounds not only of their own neighborhoods, but also of
their world—and, indeed, worlds beyond.

Colleges long ago abandoned even the pretense of the kind
of watchful care and supervision of students' personal lives that
their custodial roles once obligated them to exercise. There are
still colleges with strict rules on the consumption of alcohol and
drugs on campus, and there are still many students who observe such rules. But there are also college campuses where
liquor bottles are displayed in the windows of the dorms as

though to advertise the preferences and capacities of the inhabitants. Going to parties where alcohol is available and going to bars are popular ways for many students to have fun.

Campuses may still have rules forbidding visitation in dormitory rooms occupied by one's opposite sex. But some of these rules are honored in the breach or are not enforced, and the ongoing debates between students and administrations over whether the rules prohibiting or limiting such visitation should be rescinded accept as a premise that formal restrictions prevent little of the sexual activity students consider acceptable by their peers, and, for those who engage in it, merely make the inevitable more difficult.

During the 1960s and the 1970s, there appeared to be a strong movement of students out of institutionally controlled housing—including fraternities and sororities—and into more private living arrangements. In 1979 the U.S. Bureau of the Census reported that the percentage of students living in college housing dropped from about 30 percent in 1966 to 21 percent in 1976 ("More Collegians Living on Their Own," 1979). College residence halls lost between one-fifth and one-third of their residents to apartments or to houses other than those of the students' parents or relatives (Table 4).[3] Part of this trend is explained by the fact that many students are older and attend classes at institutions near their homes. Students at liberal arts colleges tend to remain in college-operated residence halls despite the general trend. This is largely because the resident experience is part of the tradition such colleges nourish, and much of the best they have to offer may be lost to students who live off campus. The slight shift discerned in the proportion of students in Liberal Arts Colleges II who live in their parents' homes may result from special dispensations accorded by these institutions to ease the financial burden of college attendance on the families of students who live nearby. The

[3]An increase in the percentage of community college students living in residence halls during this period probably is an anomaly associated with the newness of many of these institutions and the tendency to locate some of them in rural areas where other forms of housing are not available.

Table 4. Place of residence of undergraduates, 1969 and 1976, by percentage of undergraduates living in selected types of housing, by Carnegie classification

	Research Universities		Doctorate-granting Institutions		Comprehensive Colleges and Universities		Liberal Arts Colleges		Two-Year Colleges
	I	II	I	II	I	II	I	II	
College dormitory or other college-run housing									
1969	56%	52%	60%	70%	45%	55%	73%	66%	8%
1976	36	41	37	43	35	39	79	56	25
Fraternity or sorority house									
1969	9	12	6	4	3	8	10	2	0.2
1976	8	7	5	4	1	1	3	2	2
Rooming house or rented room									
1969	2	2	1	2	3	5	1	2	2
1976	3	1	2	2	2	2	1	1	5
At parents' home or other relatives									
1969	21	22	14	17	10	20	9	7	41
1976	11	13	14	20	29	33	6	18	12
Apartment or house (not relatives)									
1969	11	9	16	36	38	10	7	20	40
1976	40	34	39	31	31	21	11	22	51
Other									
1969	2	3	2	2	2	3	1	3	9
1976	2	3	3	1	3	3	1	2	6

Source: Carnegie Surveys, 1969-70, 1975-76.

substantial increase in the percentage of students at colleges and universities who live at home probably reflects the fact that some of these institutions were deliberately planned to provide educational opportunities within commuting distance of existing concentrations of people.

There have been scattered reports recently that fraternity and sorority memberships are on the rise and that the residence halls are filling up again. This could be part of a return to the collegiate tradition that also has been heralded on some campuses. But it could also be the result of students' discovering that the quality of life made possible by college-operated residence halls and dining commons is often superior to that which independent students can provide for themselves.

This is not to suggest, however, that students of the 1970s are seeking a return to dependence on their institutions for the discipline of their personal behavior. They remain considerably more liberal in matters of lifestyle than previous generations. For example, an increasing percentage of entering freshmen believe that marijuana should be legalized (49.5 percent in 1978 versus 25.6 percent in 1969), and divorce laws liberalized (48.6 percent in 1978 versus 41.6 percent in 1969). In addition, 45.8 percent of the 1978 freshmen think people should live together before marriage, 48.6 percent believe sexual relations are all right if people like each other, 53.7 percent believe abortion should be legalized, and 72.7 percent indicate that women's activities are not best limited to the home (Astin, King, and Richardson, 1978; Creager and others, 1969).

After a recital of these trends toward freedom from conformity and control, one is tempted to conclude that the students of the 1970s are nothing but self-indulgent. Where does the seriousness come in? At least one place it comes in is beyond the surface manifestations of the new freedom to the awesome moral and ethical burdens that go with its exercise. If students are considered serious, it is not just because their educational and career objectives are more serious than they once were, but also because they are assuming (sometimes well and sometimes not) enormous responsibilities for their own actions, that previous college generations avoided entirely or shared with their families and their institutions.

The Decline of Political Activism

The fact that newspaper headlines are not (as this is written) screaming about one student disturbance after another is cause for quiet jubilation on the nation's campuses.

The number and intensity of student protests is down at 70 percent of the institutions covered by the Carnegie Surveys of 1978. There has also been a dramatic change in the types of student protest experienced by colleges and universities in 1969 and 1977:

	Percentage of institutions experiencing protest	
	1969	*1977*
Intentional destruction of property	11.6%	1.0%
Takeover of a building	15.4	0.8
Threats of violence	20.3	2.9
Strike	13.9	1.0
Demonstration	39.2	12.8
Petition of redress	23.8	19.6
Refusal to pay tuition	0.4	0.2
Taking an issue to court	4.1	5.6
Other activities	3.5	27.4

Source: Carnegie Council Surveys, 1978.

No one knows for sure why the change occurred, but speculation embraces such possibilities as the defusing of major issues with the end of the Vietnam war and the end of compulsory selective service; progress in extending civil rights to members of minority groups; and the shock that came with the realization that the loss of student lives in May 1970 and the destruction of campus property as a protest tactic were excessive and perhaps unnecessary prices to pay for the successes that could be attributed directly to violent activism.

The thesis that the defusing of major political issues caused a decline in student protests was tested early in 1980 when President Carter proposed the registration of the nation's youth for military service. The announcement was promptly followed by many campus demonstrations in opposition to the proposal.

It is also possible that students were distracted from political endeavors as they became increasingly aware that jobs for college graduates were becoming less plentiful and that their future careers might depend on academic efforts of the most serious kind.

Finally, as can be seen in Table 5, students are becoming more conservative politically than they were in 1969-70. In 1969, 5 percent of the nation's undergraduates judged themselves to be politically "left," and 40 percent considered themselves to be "liberal." By 1976 those proportions had shrunk: Only 3 percent of the students considered themselves "left," and 39 percent considered themselves either "moderately" or "strongly" conservative. The institutions with the greatest percentage of conservative students are Liberal Arts Colleges I and Doctorate-Granting Universities I. The former include many institutions affiliated with politically conservative religious denominations. The latter are heavily concentrated in the southeast, southwest, and middle states of the country—all of which tend to be more conservative politically than other regions.

Student Participation in Governance

Students in the 1960s were preoccupied with external events and issues; students of the 1970s were moved to protest by internal issues. One of those issues is the extent to which students should have a voice in the governance of colleges and universities.

About one-half of the presidents responding to the Carnegie Council Surveys of institutional adaptations in the 1970s (1978) indicate that a substantial minority of their students are interested in (1) greater student participation in administrative decision making (for example, budgeting, fund raising, planning, and use of facilities) and (2) greater student participation in academic decision making (for example, on faculty appointments and promotion and on curriculum). About one-third of the presidents indicate that student interest in participation has decreased.

In the Carnegie Council's national survey of 1976, undergraduates divided about evenly in favoring forms of participation, including "voting power on committees," "formal consultation," "informal consultation," and "little or no role"

Table 5. Undergraduate characterization of their political orientations, by percentage of respondents by Carnegie classification, 1969 and 1975-76

	Research Universities		Doctorate-granting Institutions		Comprehensive Colleges and Universities		Liberal Arts Colleges		Two-Year Colleges	All Institutions
	I	II	I	II	I	II	I	II		
Left										
1969	10	7	5	6	4	4	10	5	3	5
1976	6	3	4	4	3	2	8	2	3	3
Liberal										
1969	48	42	39	50	40	43	47	41	35	40
1976	41	33	32	35	32	35	40	29	35	32
Middle of the road										
1969	28	32	36	31	37	39	28	36	41	37
1976	34	39	34	40	40	42	35	38	41	39
Moderately conservative										
1969	12	17	19	11	18	13	14	17	18	17
1976	17	22	26	19	22	19	15	28	18	23
Strongly conservative										
1969	2	2	2	1	2	1	2	2	2	2
1976	2	3	4	3	3	3	3	3	2	3

Source: Carnegie Surveys, 1969-70, 1975-76.

in such matters as faculty appointment and promotion, undergraduate admissions, and bachelor's degree requirements. In the matter of provision and content of courses, however, the proportion of students that said undergraduates should have "little or no role" dropped from about 20 percent to 10 percent, with almost all of this difference shifting to a preference for "formal consultation."

In 1978, 35.7 percent of the college presidents responding to the Carnegie Council's survey indicate that the influence of student government on campus policy and operations has increased since 1969-70. In addition, 23.4 percent say that individual students have increased influence. In our visits to campuses, we found that there is considerable variation in student influence, but that in an era in which the user of educational services has a lot to say about how much, when, and how services are to be provided, student preferences are receiving more serious attention. On some campuses, the structure of governance has been revised to give students strong representation on almost all administrative and academic committees, and there is a tendency for presidents to cultivate student support and use student preferences as arguments for their own objectives and policies. On such campuses, the students have more power in many respects than do the faculty or even the governing boards.

Student Satisfaction

As was noted by The Carnegie Foundation for the Advancement of Teaching (1977, p. 90):

> Even at the peak of student dissent, students who were either "satisfied" or "very satisfied" with their colleges was high (66 percent). Since that time, the level of satisfaction has remained high and has even increased slightly. In 1976, 72 percent of the nation's undergraduates reported that they were either "satisfied" or "very satisfied" with their colleges. Generally speaking, the increased satisfaction appears to reflect a relaxation of campus tensions and recent efforts of

many colleges, perhaps because of competition for enrollments, to relax requirements and introduce programs and methods that appeal to undergraduates.

That account went on to indicate that satisfaction was greatest at selective liberal arts colleges and lowest among the least comprehensive colleges and among doctorate-granting universities that awarded relatively few Ph.D.'s.

One does not have to ignore the challenge of making college and university attendance more satisfying for the 28 percent of the students who did not find it so in 1976 to appreciate the achievement of colleges and universities these responses confirm. To satisfy 76 percent of the nation's student body our colleges have to be doing at least some things right.

Graduate Students

Graduate students are yesterday's undergraduates and share some of the undergraduates' characteristics. But a few differences set them apart.

They are older, for instance. Even with the increased enrollment of undergraduates who are 25 and older, the median age of prebaccalaureate students is about 21; for graduate students it is between 26 and 27 (Carnegie Surveys, 1975-76). They have, on the average, a record of high academic ability and achievement. The fact that they have persisted in higher education for the time required to earn a bachelor's degree and have qualified for admission to selective postgraduate studies guarantees as much.

In absolute numbers, graduate students are more plentiful than they were in 1970 when there were 816 thousand of them. But the increase to 1.3 million by 1978 was not as dramatic as the enrollment increases in undergraduate divisions (NCES, 1972, 1979). One reason for this is that much of the undergraduate enrollment increase occurred in two-year colleges, where virtually no graduate programs exist. One consequence of this difference is that there has been a slight decline in the graduate student share of total enrollment—from 12.6 percent in 1970 to 11.7 percent in 1978 (NCES, 1979).

In 1969 and again in 1976, graduate students participating in a national survey were asked about their career expectations after completing their studies. In both years, teaching in elementary or secondary school, teaching or engaging in research at a college or university, or some form of professional activity dominated the choices made (Table 6). But during the 1970s

Table 6. Expectations of graduate students upon completing graduate school, 1969 and 1975, in percentages

	1969	1976
Teaching—elementary or secondary school	13.2%	20.0%
Executive or administrator in education	4.8	6.4
Teaching—junior college level	5.2	3.7
Teaching/research—college or university	28.5	17.5
Non-faculty research at a university	2.5	0.7
Research with a nonprofit organization	2.1	2.0
Research in industry	6.2	2.9
Self-employed professional practice	0.0	7.7
Professional practice alone	2.4	0.0
Professional practice with partners	5.4	0.0
Employed professional	11.8	21.6
Self-employed, business	1.4	1.1
Executive or administrator in government	2.0	3.5
Executive or administrator in business or industry	7.2	6.7
Manual or faculty work	0.1	0.1
Military service	2.0	1.3
Clerical or sales work	0.2	0.2
Other	5.1	3.9
None		0.7

Source: Carnegie Surveys, 1969-70, 1975-76.

two important shifts occurred in the most frequently mentioned options. With the well-advertised decline in college enrollments coupled with declining federal support for university research on the horizon, the percentage of graduate students expecting to work in colleges and universities decreased from 36.2 to 21.9. Some of the decrease in expectations to work in a higher education setting is offset by an increase in the proportion of graduate students expecting to teach in elementary or secondary schools. That is surprising because this sector of education expected to experience a decline in enrollment and cutbacks in resources before such changes became widespread at universities and colleges. Another part of the explanation for increased interest in teacher training, however, may lie in the fact that the percentage of women enrolled in graduate school increased from 31 to 42 between 1969 and 1976 (Table 7), and much of this increase in women's enrollments came in comprehensive colleges and universities and liberal arts colleges, all of which are traditionally committed to teacher training.

The other direction of the shift in career expectations of graduate students leads into professional practice—alone, with partners, or in the employ of a company (Table 6). The percentage of graduate students expecting to become professionals increased from 19.6 to 29.3 percent.

This general trend toward a decline in interest in academic careers is also indicated by shifts in the fields of study graduate students choose to devote themselves to. In the more academic fields, such as foreign languages, letters, mathematics, physical sciences, and the social sciences, enrollments have been declining (Table 8). But Table 8 shows substantial increases in enrollments in business and management, communications, public affairs and service, and the health professions.

Members of ethnic groups have not greatly increased their share of graduate enrollments between 1969 and 1976 (Table 9). This is a little surprising because there were affirmative action programs in existence at 40 percent of the nation's colleges and universities by 1975, and such programs have been adopted at another 50 percent of them since that time (Carnegie Council Surveys, 1978).

Politically, graduate students appear to have drifted to the left (Table 10) at the very time that undergraduates were drifting to the middle-of-the-road and to the right (Table 5). This trend cannot be explained totally in terms of either intellectual changes in individuals or the influences of external events, such as the end of the Vietnam war, economic depression, or political scandals. The shift probably reflects the fact that many of the graduate students of 1975 were under-

Table 7. Male and female graduate students as percentage of total in American colleges and universities, 1969 and 1975, by Carnegie classification

	Research Universities		Doctorate-granting Institutions		Comprehensive Colleges and Universities		Liberal Arts Colleges		Total*
	I	II	I	II	I	II	I	II	
1969 (N = 32,693)									
Male	73	74	76	77	57	48	50	64	69
Female	27	26	24	23	43	52	50	36	31
1975 (N = 25,000)									
Male	66	64	63	57	50	47	21	30	58
Female	34	36	37	43	50	53	79	70	42

*Total includes two-year colleges and specialized and technical institutions not shown elsewhere in this table.
Source: Carnegie Surveys, 1969-70, 1975-76.

Table 8. Enrollment for master's and doctor's degrees,
by field of study, 1970 and 1976

	1970 (N = 816,200)		1976 N = 1,030,000		Percentage increase or (decrease)
	Number	Percentage	Number	Percentage	
Agriculture and natural resources	10,400	1.2%	15,200	1.4%	46%
Architecture and environmental design	5,400	.7	10,100	.9	98
Area studies	2,300	.3	4,000	.4	74
Biological sciences	36,500	4.5	44,000	4.2	21
Business and management	47,500	5.8	150,000	16.6	215
Communications	2,500	.3	8,800	.9	252
Computer and information sciences	7,900	.9	11,900	1.1	51
Education	257,600	31.6	324,500	31.5	26
Engineering	64,800	7.9	57,300	5.6	(12)
Fine and applied arts	19,900	2.4	30,200	2.9	52
Foreign languages	18,600	2.3	12,800	1.2	(31)
Health professions	14,200	1.7	38,100	3.7	168
Home economics	4,600	.6	8,100	.8	76
Law	2,500	.3	3,600	.3	44
Letters	51,200	6.3	44,000	4.3	(14)
Library science	12,400	1.5	13,300	1.3	7
Mathematics	22,700	2.8	14,900	1.4	(34)
Physical sciences	40,100	4.9	36,100	3.5	(9)
Psychology	25,300	3.0	35,400	3.4	40
Public affairs and service	19,700	2.4	53,000	5.1	169
Social sciences	76,800	9.4	67,100	6.5	(12)
Theology	7,200	.9	10,800	1.0	50
Interdisciplinary studies	26,100	3.2	30,700	3.0	18

Source: Adapted from NCES, 1978a, p. 90.

Table 9. Members of racial or ethnic groups as a percentage of graduate student enrollment in American colleges and universities, 1969 and 1975, by Carnegie classification

	Research Universities		Doctorate-granting Institutions		Comprehensive Colleges and Universities		Liberal Arts Colleges		Total
	I	II	I	II	I	II	I	II	
White/Caucasian									
1969	93%	94%	88%	94%	93%	96%	94%	99%	93%
1975	89	90	87	92	91	92	96	52	90
Black									
1969	2	1	5	1	4	1	1	0	2
1975	3	3	6	3	4	6	2	45	5
Oriental/other Asian									
1969	4	3	5	3	2	1	5	1	3
1975	5	6	5	3	3	1	1	1	3
Native American									
1969	*	*	*	*	*	*	*	*	*
1975	0	0	0	0	0	1	1	0	0
Mexican American									
1969	*	*	*	*	*	*	*	*	*
1975	1	0	1	1	1	0	0	0	1
Puerto Rican									
1969	*	*	*	*	*	*	*	*	*
1975	0	0	0	0	0	0	1	0	0
Other									
1969	2	1	3	2	1	1	0	0	2
1975	2	1	2	1	1	1	0	2	1

*Data not available.
Source: Carnegie Surveys, 1969-70, 1975-76.

Table 10. Responses of graduate students to the question "How would you characterize yourself politically at the present time?" In percentages, 1969, 1975, by Carnegie classification

	Research Universities		Doctorate-granting Institutions		Comprehensive Colleges and Universities		Liberal Arts Colleges		Total*
	I	II	I	II	I	II	I	II	
Left									
1969	9	5	4	4	3	1	12	0	6
1975	12	7	9	5	4	3	13	2	7
Liberal									
1969	44	36	36	34	31	26	31	31	37
1975	46	42	37	35	30	29	43	42	37
Middle-of-the-road									
1969	24	28	26	29	30	31	28	30	27
1975	24	28	30	29	34	35	24	27	30
Moderately conservative									
1969	20	28	29	29	32	37	27	36	28
1975	16	20	23	28	29	31	18	27	24
Strongly conservative									
1969	2	3	4	5	4	4	2	4	4
1975	2	3	3	4	3	3	2	3	3

*Totals include two-year colleges, and specialized and technical institutions not included elsewhere in this table.
Source: Carnegie Surveys, 1969-70, 1975-76.

graduates during the 1960s and apparently brought their political commitments with them when they acquired their new status. In the same way, by as early as 1980, it is reasonable for us to expect that the dominant political orientation of graduate students will be more moderate and conservative— reflecting the orientations of the undergraduates in the late 1970s.

Whatever their political attitudes may be, graduate students are in remarkable agreement that their institutions are at least "fairly good" places for them to be. More than 90 percent expressed that view in both 1969 and 1975 (Table 11). There was some decline, however, in the percentage that say their institution is "a very good place" for them to be, and the reasons for the change are not entirely clear. One of them, certainly, is that the prospects for academic employment of persons with advanced degrees are not as good as they were in 1969. Another is that there may be some curtailment of financial assistance through cutbacks of fellowships and teaching and research assistanceships.

Concluding Observations

One of the difficulties in interpreting the abundant data that have been collected by the Carnegie Commission on Higher Education, the Carnegie Council, and others about student characteristics and attitudes is that it is not always possible to know which changes derive from the lives and needs of the students themselves and which derive from changes in institutional policies. These difficulties are particularly acute in an era in which students, on the one hand, discover that they have considerable power over institutions of higher learning just by exercising one of the many options that are available to them; and in which institutions, on the other hand, feel compelled to adjust their programs in order to attract and hold students as one of their survival strategies.

Originally, the recruitment and enrollment of the disadvantaged, members of ethnic minorities, and women had a rationale rooted primarily in enlightened attitudes about social justice. However, the nobility of such efforts was diluted at

Table 11. Percentage of graduate students expressing satisfaction or dissatisfaction with their colleges and universities, 1969 and 1975, by Carnegie classification

	Research Universities		Doctorate-granting Institutions		Comprehensive Colleges and Universities		Liberal Arts Colleges		Two-Year Colleges	All institutions*
	I	II	I	II	I	II	I	II		
It is a very good place for me.										
1969	53%	50%	44%	47%	49%	51%	58%	59%	30%	50%
1975	42	37	37	39	38	39	57	49	37	39
It is a fairly good place for me.										
1969	41	44	48	46	45	45	35	39	62	44
1975	50	53	55	53	55	54	40	43	54	53
It is not the place for me.										
1969	6	6	7	7	6	4	6	1	7	6
1975	8	10	8	8	7	7	4	8	9	8

*Includes specialized institutions and technical institutions now shown elsewhere in this table.

Source: Carnegie Surveys, 1969-70, 1975-76.

some institutions, who introduced and refashioned them primarily to avoid federal penalties for inadequate affirmative
action to end discrimination. Expanding educational opportunities took on yet another cast when institutions felt compelled not only to increase admissions of members of formerly
excluded groups in our society, but also to actively seek them
out and entice them to their campuses as a means of maintaining attendance levels.

The phenomenon of the older student is only partially
explained by societal changes and new motivations for individual
learners. It also has to be explained in terms of institutional efforts to recruit older students in order to cushion the plummet-
ing enrollments of students of the traditional 17- to 24-year-old
variety. The emergence of off-campus centers, evening colleges,
and special, occupationally oriented master's-degree programs at
former liberal arts institutions is part of this pattern. And these
new efforts could have an important influence on the shape of
education in the 1980s and 1990s.

The term *student consumerism* was introduced in the
1970s to describe the way students influence changes in higher
education by their choices among the many options available
to them. The aptness of the term is widely debated. It offends
those who consider higher education to be totally unlike anything else on earth and therefore exempt from metaphorical
description. It also offends those who tend to think of educated
people—ex-students, if you will—as the real products of education. For them, the notion of a product being its own consumer is untenable. It also offends those who fear the loss of
institutional authority implicit in "the customer is always
right" features of the consumer metaphor. The strongest
advocates of the consumerist concept are those who think of
education—portions of knowledge of various kinds packaged
in certain sizes and shapes—as a product for which students
pay money. And the payment of money is presumed to endow
students with a degree of sovereignty. Whether or not the
metaphor is apt, the process envisioned by those of the consumerist persuasion is real. It actually happens, and it is no
longer (if it ever was) appropriate to think of the higher

education experience as a standardized, fixed thing that is either in or out of demand depending upon a few superficial characteristics of a given student generation.

Those who shape educational policy also have choices to make, however, and anyone who views the situation entirely from the student's point of view may miss an important part of the dynamics of consumerism. For by making decisions about what they will offer to satisfy student demand, presidents, deans, and faculty members who shape educational policy also alter the characteristics of the student bodies they choose to serve. The clumsy addition of certain kinds of vocational programs to a liberal arts curriculum ultimately could have as much effect on the character of a college's student body as making a single-sex institution coeducational.

My final observation on students is that most of the available information about them is of a variety that helps us to understand their numbers, their socioeconomic status, their attitudes toward certain events and issues, their sexual characteristics, and their ethnic variety. All of these variables are interesting and do shed light on the dynamics of educational policy and planning, but they do little to help us understand educational quality and the effectiveness of instructional techniques. College and university teachers who ask how the presence of older students, women students, and students from racial minorities should affect their teaching strategies are asking what may, in the long run, be the most important question to be asked about the significance of the changing national student body. Unfortunately, the answers we can supply thus far are too often inferred from stereotypes about the interests and educability of members of these groups. It is too often forgotten that other variables may be more important to the learning process. Some people learn fast, some learn slowly. Some deal best with abstractions, others are more comfortable with the concrete. Some are lazy, some are eager. Some learn best by reading, others learn best by listening—or writing. Although we can make a great deal of progress educationally by just making sure that no one is needlessly or thoughtlessly left out when we close the college doors, that may not be enough. We are coming to a point in the history of higher education when we have to pay more attention to helping everyone who gets into a classroom realize the best possible results from their learning potentials. Achieving that goal may require more studies of the subtle and profound differences and changes in the characteristics of students than we have so far been prepared to consider making to improve higher educational policy.

3

Faculty

American academics may be the most systematically and frequently studied of all professionals. They were examined in considerable detail in national surveys conducted by the Carnegie Commission on Higher Education in 1969, the Carnegie Council in 1975, the American Council on Education in 1973 (Bayer, 1973), and E. C. Ladd and S. M. Lipset in 1973 and again in 1975 (1976). They have been the subject of several books and of a series of extensive articles in the *Chronicle of Higher Education* (Ladd and Lipset, 1976).[1]

Ladd and Lipset (1976) explain this great interest in terms of the "expanded roles" of the members of the American professoriate and their technical-scientific-intellectual kin in a knowledge-powered American society. As far as it goes, that assessment is correct. But, there is more to be said, and it is traceable to the belief, perhaps romantic, of many people that teachers plant pieces of themselves in the lives of those they teach and thus are in a unique position to influence the conduct of future generations. Such power is awesome, and those who have it seem to owe it to the rest of us to satisfy our curiosity about them.

An educator from a South American country recently asked me why American academics seemed to be so pessimistic

---

[1]This series was published in the *Chronicle of Higher Education* between September 15, 1975, and May 31, 1976. Reprints of the series were produced by the Social Science Data Center at the University of Connecticut, Storrs, under the title, *The Character and Opinions of the American Professoriate.*

and cynical. Without knowing exactly what kind of academics she had met, a definitive answer was impossible. I share her impression, however, that the mood of American college and university faculty members has darkened during the 1970s. And there are many reasons:

- The philosophical validity of the scientific method and of the objectivity of academic inquiry began to be questioned in the 1960s. Whether they participate in the debate or not, the question still lurks in the profound levels of the consciousness of many academics.

- Harnessing nuclear energy, landing a man on the moon, and computerizing much of the daily lives of the members of industrial societies are tough acts to follow. They are also accompanied by hazards to the quality of life and the health of mankind. Moreover, the persistence of war, the pollution of the environment, and the waste of natural resources—not to mention crime and disease—force a new humility upon those who only a few decades ago were overly optimistic about the power of knowledge and science to improve the human condition.

- On the campuses, the student revolts of the 1960s seemed at first to be directed at college and university leaders—presidents, trustees, and administrators—against whom faculty members also were inclined to hold grievances. Some faculty members were surprised to find that students considered them to be as remote and uncaring as their leaders, but faculty members who embraced the platforms of the student protesters were also surprised by the antagonism of some of their colleagues.

- As faculty members began to take sides, they exposed what Martin Trow (1975) calls the "private life" of the academic sector to view and criticism. One consequence of the unprecedented national preoccupation with higher education in the 1970s—in the form of national commissions and task forces that were engaged in studies of its structure, governance, and financing—is that the idealistic view of the American faculty member as self-sacrificing, inspired, unworldly, wise, and unfalteringly benevolent changed. Campuses came to be described in terms of power politics and competition for students and resources. The strategies required for advancement in an academic career were exposed and often misinterpreted. This "real life" perspective, underscored by the growth of the movement to unionize college and university faculties, emphasizes bread-and-butter issues and deemphasizes the faculty members' dedication and concern for the life of the mind and the enrichment of the national culture. In 1975, Ladd and Lipset (1976) reported that two out of three professors believe that the status of the academic profession has declined.

• This perception of declining professional status was not improved by the evidence offered by A. Cartter (1975) and reasserted by L. Fernandez (1978) that the number of faculty positions needed in American colleges and universities will decline as institutions try to adjust to diminished resources and declining enrollments. Faculty members have found that the academic enterprise is no longer expanding and that, as a result, they are losing some of their bargaining power in negotiating with current and potential employers.

• Faculty salaries have failed to keep up with the cost of living. Although some faculty members at major institutions are paid very well, the average salary for faculty members in all ranks and in all kinds of institutions in 1978-79 is $19,300 per year. Salaries are highest ($21,700) at universities, and lowest ($18,300) at two-year colleges. The annual rate of increase in salaries between 1969-70 and 1978-79 was 5.2 percent, although in the later year the rate is reported as 6.2 percent by the National Center for Education Statistics. Meanwhile, the Consumer Price Index (CPI) increased by 9 percent between December 1977 and December 1978 ("Cost of Living Outpaces Year's Rise in Pay," 1979, p. 12).

• Faculty members who happen to be women have an additional complaint. In all ranks, a significant differential between the average salaries earned by men and those earned by women continues. In 1976-77, for example, male professors on nine-month contracts earned $2,500 more, on the average, than did women with the same rank. The differential fell to $900 for associate professors, $600 for assistant professors, and $500 for instructors (NCES, 1978a, p. 98). In the future, these differentials should decrease as women hired in accordance with affirmative action policies initiated in the 1970s gradually gain seniority within their ranks. But it will not be eliminated entirely until some of the most highly paid male faculty members die or retire.

All of these factors notwithstanding, Ladd and Lipset warn that it would be a mistake to paint a picture of an unhappy professoriate. For example, in 1975, 87 percent of the American faculty members said if they had to do it over again they would still answer "definitely" or "probably" to an academic career (Ladd and Lipset, 1976). Ladd and Lipset fail to note, however, that this was a decrease from the 92 percent of the faculty who gave the same answers in the Carnegie surveys conducted five years earlier (Carnegie Surveys, 1969).

The Growth of Faculties

When enrollment increases, the size of college and university faculties also increase, and that situation prevailed throughout the 1970s. In 1969, there were 546,000 persons employed as either full-time or part-time faculty members at colleges and universities in the United States. By 1976, the number had increased to 781,000 (NCES, 1978a, p. 104).

These increases did not, however, occur uniformly in institutions of higher education. Officials at 59 percent of the colleges and universities report to the Carnegie Council that there was an increase of more than 10 percent in the absolute number of instructional faculty from 1969-70 to 1977-78 (Table 12), but 27 percent report little or no change, and 14 percent report a decrease of 10 percent or more. The institutions that most frequently report increases in the size of their

Table 12. Percentage of institutions indicating changes in the absolute number of total instructional staff members from 1969-70 to 1977-78, by Carnegie classification

	Research Universities		Doctorate-granting Institutions		Comprehensive Colleges and Universities		Liberal Arts Colleges		Two-Year Colleges	Total
	I	II	I	II	I	II	I	II		
Increase over 10 percent	44%	66%	65%	37%	64%	48%	22%	43%	74%	59%
Little or no change	48	28	40	48	20	35	61	37	17	27
Decrease over 10 percent	9	6	19	15	16	17	17	21	10	14

Source: Carnegie Council Surveys, 1978.

Table 13. Percentage of institutions expecting changes in the absolute number of total instructional staff members from 1977-78 to 1985-86, by Carnegie classification

	Research Universities		Doctorate-granting Institutions		Comprehensive Colleges and Universities		Liberal Arts Colleges		Two-Year Colleges	Total
	I	II	I	II	I	II	I	II		
Increase over 10 percent	2%	21%	19%	16%	21%	26%	9%	32%	48%	35%
Little or no change	79	67	66	84	63	61	81	62	48	57
Decrease over 10 percent	19	12	15	0	17	13	9	6	4	8

Source: Carnegie Council Surveys, 1978.

instructional staff are those in classifications that include large numbers of new institutions and those that are particularly likely to experience enrollment growth. These are the two-year colleges, the comprehensive colleges and universities, and some of the research and doctorate-granting universities.

In the years ahead, officials at 48 percent of the two-year colleges expect to increase their faculties by 10 percent, and 32 percent of the Liberal Arts II colleges have similar expectations (Table 13). But most of the colleges and universities in all classifications expect little or no change in the absolute numbers of instructional staff members. In fact, officials at 8 percent of them expect the size of their faculties to decrease by 10 percent or more in the first half of the 1980s.

Participation of Women and Minorities

The dominance of white males on college and university faculties is slowly eroding. Between 1969 and 1975, the percentage of women among faculty members increased from 20 to 25 percent (Carnegie Surveys, 1969-70, 1975-76). Members of minorities also made modest gains. Black faculty increased from 2.9 percent in 1972 (Carnegie Council on Policy Studies in Higher Education, 1975a, p. 39) to 4 percent in 1976 (NCES, 1978d, p. 194). The percentage of orientals and other members of minorities, however, remained at a level of approximately 2 percent during this period.

Faculty Responses to Affirmative Action

The Carnegie Council on Policy Studies in Higher Education began its report, *Making Affirmative Action Work in Higher Education* (1975a, p. 1), with the following observations:

> The historical record of many institutions of higher education in employing, promoting, and paying women and members of minority groups has been grossly inadequate in meeting the test of equality of opportunity.
>
> Substantial progress has recently been made, however, and further progress is now being made by many institutions.

Affirmative action, nevertheless, is needed to overcome the residue of a past record of discrimination which was partially purposive and partially inadvertent. It will be needed until a better record of nondiscrimination has been established, a situation where there is nondiscrimination on the basis of sex, race, and ethnic origin, and discrimination only on the basis of ability and contribution to institutional needs.

The 1970s were, in fact, years of historic efforts in colleges and universities to redress some of the imbalances in the participation of women and members of minority groups in higher education. Some of the efforts were voluntary. Some were made under the pressure of national civil rights legislation and governmental regulation. The results, on the whole, have been a modest success.

Given an opportunity to react to some of the issues raised by this national effort, faculty members responded as follows:

Proposition	Percentage agreeing[a]	Percentage disagreeing[b]
The normal academic requirements should be relaxed in appointing members of minority groups to the faculty here	12%	88%
Issues raised by affirmative action are causing serious strains among the faculty in my department	23	77
Affirmative action is unfair to white males	50	50
On the whole, women have not been discriminated against in academic life	21	79
American colleges are racist whether they mean to be or not	44	56
Affirmative action labels members of minority groups in such a way that they can never be judged on merit alone	56	44

[a]Includes responses of "strongly agree" and "agree with reservations."
[b]Includes responses of "strongly disagree" and "disagree with reservations."
Source: Carnegie Surveys, 1975-76.

At the risk of oversimplifying the significance of these responses (and without pretending that they even begin to exhaust all of the issues affirmative action raises), I would summarize them this way: American academics disagree with many of the premises on which affirmative action is based and are defensive about the extent to which their institutions may be discriminatory in academic personnel matters. They are at least consenting, however, when it comes to the measures institutions may have to take to correct the imbalance of opportunities that exists for women and members of minorities on college faculties. The presidents of American colleges and universities hold views similar to those of the faculty. In 1978, 85 percent of them disagree, either strongly or with reservations, that "The faculty members at this institution are beginning to resist efforts to hire more women and members of minorities on our academic staff" (Carnegie Council Surveys, 1978).

Part-Time Faculty

I recently heard a story about an English instructor who divided his teaching time among two state university campuses and a two-year community college, all located within 100 miles of each other. He meets classes at one college in the mornings, at another in the afternoons, and has time on alternate days or in the evenings for the third. Although the arrangement lacks job security, the comforts of a permanent base of operations, and other benefits associated with a full-time position, it does offer the instructor some independence and exempts him from much of the committee work and other routines to which college professors must devote time. The combined revenue of the three positions is apparently sufficient to his needs.

Colleges and universities are finding part-time faculty members attractive. They teach only courses in the basic curriculum and not those that full-time faculty members with special interests are sometimes allowed to teach. Their employment involves no commitment by the institution to support their research. They are not on the academic "ladder" and thus can be rewarded or discharged with none of the investment of time often spent in the hiring and promotion of regular faculty members. They require a minimum of office space and staff support.

In May 1979, the *Chronicle of Higher Education* published an article by P. Lauter, a professor at the State University of New York College at Old Westbury, on the growing practice of hiring part-time professors. He estimates the economic incentives of hiring part-time faculty members as follows (p. 72):

> My college . . . had about 87 full-time and 53 part-time or adjunct faculty members in 1977-78. Adjuncts average about $1,000 per course (which is, in fact, fairly good for this kind of work on Long Island). They taught some 55 courses, at an approximate cost to the institution of $55,000. Had the courses been taught by full-time faculty members of comparable appointment levels, the cost to the institution would have been approximately $2,500 per course, or a total of $137,500, just for the base salary. To that, one must add roughly 30 percent for benefits for full-timers, none of which the adjuncts get. The total cost would have been $178,750. In short, by having those 55 courses taught by adjuncts, the College at Old Westbury "saved" about $123,750.

It is not clear that all institutions that employ part-time faculty achieve economies of this magnitude, but it is clear that the percentage of part-time faculty members on the total instructional staff of colleges and universities is increasing. In 1969 part-time staff members constituted an estimated 22 percent of the total instructional staff at the level of instructor and above in all colleges and universities in the United States. In 1976 the percentage had risen to 31, and in 1978 it is estimated to be 32 percent. Among junior instructional staff, the percentage (84) was much higher in 1976, but it now appears to be holding steady or even decreasing slightly (NCES, 1978a).

In the Carnegie Council Surveys of 1978, an increase in the number of part-time faculty as a percentage of total faculty since 1969-70 is reported by 56 percent of the Two-Year Colleges, 51 percent of the Comprehensive Universities and Colleges II, and 50 percent of the Liberal Arts Colleges II.

Some of this increase involves the external occupational and professional programs offered by these institutions at nights, on weekends, and at off-campus locations. About one-third of these same types of institutions expect to increase the use of part-time faculty members between 1977-78 and 1985-86 (Carnegie Council Surveys, 1978). However, most institutions of all kinds expect little or no change in the ratio of part-time to full-time faculty.

Faculty Age

The faculty of American colleges and universities is getting older. Although the age ranges differ slightly in the two columns, the following table (based on Carnegie Surveys, 1969-70 and 1975-76) illustrates the change.

Range in years	Percentage in 1969	Range in years	Percentage in 1975
61 or more	8%	60 or more	10%
51-60	16	50-59	19
46-50	13	45-49	13
41-45	15	40-44	14
36-40	17	35-39	18
31-35	17	30-34	14
30 and under	13	29 and under	11

The faculty could be still older 10 years from now as those hired to accommodate the increasing enrollments in the 1960s who are now in the 30- to 40-year-old age range obtain tenure.

The Quality of Faculty

When asked what has happened to the quality of faculty members at their institutions since 1970 (Carnegie Council Surveys, 1978), college and university presidents respond as follows:

Quality enhanced	67.5%
Quality both enhanced and impaired	17.4
No change	11.1
Don't know	1.1

The presidents who say that the quality of their faculty is enhanced cite three basic reasons: the institution of faculty development programs to improve the teaching of faculty members already on the staff (37 percent); better preparation (30 percent); and (what probably amounts to the same thing) more faculty with Ph.D.'s (28 percent). The truth is that colleges and universities have been reveling in a buyer's market when it comes to acquiring academic talent. There is an ample supply of qualified teachers and scholars in most fields, and many of them are looking for jobs at institutions that might not have appealed to them when openings were more plentiful. Some of the new faculty members have a recently instituted degree, the Doctor of Arts, which is designed for persons who intend to concentrate on college-level teaching rather than research. About one-fifth of all colleges and universities have hired one or more faculty members with this degree since 1969-70. But such hiring seldom takes place in either Liberal Arts Colleges I or Research Universities I, which are highly selective in their admissions policies and have reputations for offering high-quality instruction.

The emphasis on teaching in relation to research continues to reflect the orientation of the type of institution that hires the Ph.D.'s who are available. For example, interest in teaching remains strong at two-year colleges and liberal arts colleges and is fairly strong also at comprehensive colleges and universities. When faculty members themselves are asked about their interest in teaching, however, there seems to have been some slippage in that interest between 1969 and 1975 (Table 14). Only in Liberal Arts Colleges II, where 55 percent of the faculties said they were heavily interested in teaching in 1969 and 56 percent said they were heavily interested in teaching in 1975, was there no decrease in faculty interest in teaching. Even in those institutions, however, the percentage of faculty interested in teaching drops if the "very heavily interested in teaching" and "in both, but leaning toward teaching" responses are combined. For 1969 the combined percentages were 95, for 1975, they were 91. The shift is not large, but it is difficult to resist the speculation that the availability of faculty with Ph.D.'s may be skewing the interests of faculty members at what were formerly teaching-oriented institutions somewhat away from teaching. If that is

Table 14. Faculty preference for teaching or research, 1969 and 1975, in percentages, by Carnegie classification

Responses to the question: "Do your interests lie primarily in teaching or research?"	Research Universities I	II	Doctorate-granting Institutions I	II	Comprehensive Colleges and Universities I	II	Liberal Arts Colleges I	II	Two-Year Colleges	All institutions[a]
Very heavily in research										
1969	8%	7%	5%	4%	2%	1%	1%	1%	1%	3%
1975	11	8	6	4	2	1	2	1	0	4
In both, but leaning toward research										
1969	37	30	27	22	13	10	12	8	4	20
1975	43	37	33	28	16	13	16	8	6	21
In both, but leaning toward teaching										
1969	35	38	40	38	35	39	31	40	19	34
1975	33	38	41	40	43	41	43	35	24	36
Very heavily in teaching										
1969	19	25	29	36	48	54	60	55	77	43
1975	13	18	20	28	39	46	39	56	70	39

[a]The percentage for all institutions includes specialized and technical institutions not included elsewhere in this table.

Source: Carnegie Surveys, 1969-70, 1975-76.

the case, giving more emphasis to Doctor of Arts degree programs merits greater attention.

This change in interest in teaching should not be allowed to obscure the fact, however, that, except in Research Universities I (where the interests of less than one-half of the faculties even "lean" toward teaching), fairly high percentages of faculty (ranging from 56 to 94 percent) still show a preference for teaching.

Wherever their interests may lie, faculty members apparently are going to be more carefully evaluated when promotions are considered in the future. This is partly because the size of the pool of qualified applicants will probably exceed the openings for several years and partly because colleges and universities will feel that their financial resources are too limited to be invested in anything less than the best talent they can afford. The university officials who participated in the Carnegie Council Surveys of 1978 indicate that more than one-half of them tightened their standards for promoting faculty members within ranks during the 1970s, and about two-thirds expect such standards to become increasingly stiffer through the 1980s (Table 15).

Promotions to tenure will be especially difficult to get. In 1979, 63.5 percent of the faculty of American colleges and universities hold tenured positions ("Percentage of Faculty Members with Tenure," 1979, p. 14). Tenure rates of that magnitude translate into relatively few opportunities for faculty members to escape nontenure ranks—both because of the paucity of openings and the high costs of salaries, fringe benefits, and other perquisites associated with tenured positions. During the 1970s, 16 percent of the American colleges and universities placed limits on the number of tenured positions relative to total faculty size that could be sustained in the future (Carnegie Council Surveys, 1978).

Representation in Departments

One of the most difficult problems confronting academic deans at colleges and universities is matching institutional resources with student demand. That problem is well illustrated by comparing undergraduate enrollment in the various majors with the commitment of faculty members to the various departments. Figure 1 shows that, between 1969 and 1976, the percentage of students enrolled in professional or occupational majors increased from 38 to 58, while the percentage in the humanities dropped from 9 to 5. The percentage of students enrolled in the physical sciences dropped from 7 to 4. Figure 2 shows that the proportion of faculty teaching in the various departments changed much less dramatically between 1969 and 1975-76. In fact, in 1975 the configuration of faculty membership in departments more nearly matches the configuration of student enrollment in 1969 than it does that of 1975.

Figure 2. Percentage of faculty members teaching major subject fields. 1969 and 1975-76

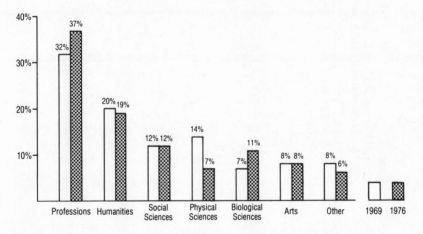

Note: Numbers may not add to 100 because of rounding.
Source: Carnegie Surveys, 1969-70, 1975-76.

The percentage of faculty members in humanities departments is almost unchanged, reflecting the role these departments play in providing the courses (foreign language, history, English, for example) that students have to take to graduate or to satisfy general education requirements. The faculty commitment to the social sciences remains unchanged from 1969 but

Table 15. Percentage of institutions engaging in selected efforts to improve faculty quality between 1969-70 and 1977-78 and expecting to make such efforts between 1977-78 and 1985-86, by Carnegie classification

	Research Universities		Doctorate-granting Institutions		Comprehensive Colleges and Universities		Liberal Arts Colleges		Two-Year Colleges	All institutions
	I	II	I	II	I	II	I	II		
Increase in systematic efforts to evaluate faculty competence										
Occurred 1969-70 to 1977-78	69%	72%	84%	68%	76%	70%	80%	84%	70%	76%
Expected 1977-78 to 1985-86	43	63	76	63	83	75	69	77	73	76
Increase in systematic efforts to retrain underutilized faculty for new or related fields or functions										
Occurred 1969-70 to 1977-78	10	16	9	22	23	23	29	35	18	23
Expected 1977-78 to 1985-86	33	63	46	50	68	67	65	66	61	63

Increase in rigor of standards for faculty salary increases									
Occurred 1969-78 to 1977-78	34	53	69	59	54	43	41	36	29	38
Expected 1977-78 to 1985-86	45	45	60	65	72	66	55	71	49	59
Increase in rigor of standards for faculty promotion in rank									
Occurred 1969-70 to 1977-78	64	74	89	90	70	70	69	57	42	58
Expected 1977-78 to 1985-86	59	59	71	68	76	70	70	65	44	60
Increase in rigor of faculty tenure standards									
Occurred 1969-70 to 1977-78	62	78	91	90	70	74	69	61	26	54
Expected 1977-78 to 1985-86	57	66	76	68	73	76	60	64	44	60

Source: Carnegie Council Surveys, 1978.

closely matches student interest in those subjects in 1975. Faculty participation in the biological sciences in 1975 exceeds what would be expected by the strength of student demand, but the increase is not too surprising. These have been increasingly attractive subjects not only for teaching, but also for research and have probably attracted some faculty members who might, in earlier times, have taught in physical science departments.

In some respects, looking at faculty subject interests from a national perspective is deceiving because the national perspective tends to reflect institutional distribution of fields of instruction as much as it represents personal student and faculty preferences. The heavy representation of the humanities, for example, is caused in part by the fact that all types of institutions—excluding those devoted entirely to specialized and professional studies—tend to offer instruction in such fields. In contrast, only some fraction of the institutions offer instruction in the physical and biological sciences, or in more than one or two subjects in the social sciences.

The fact remains, however, that there is an inevitable disjuncture between student interests and faculty resources. Student interests become known to institutional planners after the fact, and it may take several years for a college to reallocate its resources to take care of any changes in those interests. It is not simply a matter of adding faculty for a new high-interest field. More often, it is a matter of reassigning positions as they open up, from less popular departments to those with the greatest demand. Only in periods when considerable external interest in new subject fields exists—as was the case in atomic and space science after World War II—is there likely to be an infusion of new funding to provide teachers in high-demand fields.

Academic Personnel Policies in Times of Change

Colleges and universities are not likely to lay faculty members off in great numbers in order to adjust to decreasing enrollments and consequent reductions in financial resources. For one thing, tenure policies make laying people off very difficult.

For another, there are less traumatic ways to accomplish at least some of the objectives that would be met by faculty dismissals. Consequently, between 1969 and 1978, only about one-fifth of the colleges and universities inaugurated staff reduction policies that involved faculty layoffs, and about the same proportion anticipate adopting such policies in the future (Carnegie Council Surveys, 1978).

One hedge against having too many faculty members when enrollments begin to decline is to avoid hiring faculty members when enrollments are still rising. This inevitably means that the teaching load of the existing faculty will be increased. And that, in fact, has happened—at least in terms of students to faculty ratios. Between 1969 and 1978, the proportion of colleges and universities with students to faculty ratios below 17 to 1 decreased appreciably, while ratios of 18 to 1 and higher increased (Table 16).[2]

Table 16. Approximate ratios of students to faculty on college and university campuses in 1969-70 and 1977-78, by percentage of institutions

	1969-70 Percentage	1977-78 Percentage
8 to 1 or lower	4.5%	3.0%
Between 9 to 1 and 11 to 1	11.4	8.8
Between 12 to 1 and 14 to 1	23.9	18.7
Between 15 to 1 and 17 to 1	25.5	23.6
Between 18 to 1 and 20 to 1	17.6	27.1
21 to 1 or higher	17.2	18.7

Note: Numbers may not add to 100 because of rounding.
Source: Carnegie Council Surveys, 1978.

Encouraging some faculty members to take early retirement is a major change in academic personnel policy at some institutions (Table 17), aimed less at staff reduction than at decreasing academic payroll costs. It reduces the number of staff members who are at the most senior levels, where they

[2]About two-thirds (67.7 percent) of the campuses cited used the FTE measure, 28.7 percent used the headcount measure, and 3.5 percent used other methods.

Table 17. Extent of change in policies involving incentives for early retirement in colleges and universities, 1969-70 to 1977-78, in percentages of institutions, by Carnegie classification

	Research Universities		Doctorate-granting Institutions		Comprehensive Colleges and Universities		Liberal Arts Colleges		Two-Year Colleges	All institutions
	I	II	I	II	I	II	I	II		
Extent of change										
Increase										
Occurred 1969-70 to 1977-78	41%	18%	32%	41%	20%	16%	15%	3%	11%	14.0%
Expected 1977-78 to 1985-86	53	53	56	58	61	41	46	34	27	39.0
Little or no change										
Occurred 1969-70 to 1977-78	59	80	69	59	80	83	85	97	88	86.0
Expected 1977-78 to 1985-86	47	47	38	50	37	59	54	66	73	61.0
Decrease										
Occurred 1969-70 to 1977-78	0	2	0	0	0	1	0	0	2	1.0
Expected 1977-78 to 1985-86	0	0	6	4	2	0	0	0	0	0.2

Source: Carnegie Council Surveys, 1978.

tend to be most expensive. Studies have shown, however, that, although early retirements have short-term advantages, the long-range benefits, at least in terms of creating less expensive junior faculty positions, may be negligible (for example, Fernandez, 1978, p. 5). Only 14 percent of the nation's colleges and universities instituted such a policy between 1969 and 1978, although 39 percent of them expect to have such policies in effect within the next five or six years. It is clear from site visits made early in 1978, incidentally, that incentives for early retirement may be offered selectively to "problem" faculty members and to tenured faculty members in departments that experience severe enrollment decline (for example, foreign language departments). In such instances, the problem may center less on a professor's age than on the fact that he or she has tenure and cannot be dismissed except for extraordinary reasons that do not necessarily or unequivocably include an institution's retrenchment.

The institution of tenure itself, however, does not appear to be in great danger. Only about 100 institutions have abolished it since 1969-70, and no more than 62 say that they might abolish it by 1985-86 (Carnegie Council Surveys, 1978). But tenure does have critics, one of whom says that it is "inimical to academic freedom, it discourages radical innovations and risk taking, it limits the mobility of professors, and it may even work to the ultimate advantage of administrators in bargaining with professors" (O'Toole, 1978, p. 25). Tenure's defenders, however, continue to regard it as essential to the preservation of academic freedom. Asked in 1975 to indicate the extent of their agreement with the proposition that "The abolition of faculty tenure would on the whole improve the quality of American higher education," 61 percent of the faculty members responding to the Carnegie survey say they "strongly disagree" or "disagree with reservations" (Carnegie Survey, 1975).

One university official interviewed by the Carnegie Council in 1978 points out that, as a practical matter, the abolition of tenure is not a means of creating more flexibility in academic hiring policies. In fact, he observes, the tradition of tenure has become so ingrained in American higher education that it is taken for granted and its formal abolition would actually mean nothing less than the institution of "instant tenure" for everyone.

In times of retrenchment, the difficulties that attend having a "tenured-in" faculty are so acute that some college officials are exerting strong controls at the front end of the system. One college president says that, because his academic deans know that a professor acquiring tenure will be on the staff for a long time and cannot be let go without difficulty, nominees for tenure are now screened with unprecedented care. If this example is followed elsewhere, the young faculty members in the 1980s may be in a double bind. They will have to compete strenuously for the few tenured positions that open up and also must meet promotion standards that are more severe than those imposed on the tenured faculty members whose vacated positions they seek.

Faculty Governance

How faculty members are hired, promoted, given tenure, and involved in the day-to-day life of their institutions is governed largely by the way academic and administrative affairs are organized on the campuses. On relatively small campuses and at many two-year institutions, the organizational model closely resembles that of a business organization. Authority is concentrated at the top in presidents and in a few key administrators with some delegation to departments. Institutionwide participation of faculty members at such institutions tends to be sporadic and largely advisory.

At large universities and colleges and at elite institutions, the faculty members are entrusted with authority over a broad range of matters in which they are considered to hold special professional competence. Among them are degree requirements, the shape of the curriculum, and policies for the appointment and promotion of academic personnel.

Even in institutions where traditions of strong faculty government prevail, only a small portion of the faculty actually takes part. Baldridge and his associates learned in their

1978 surveys that only 18 percent of the faculty members consider themselves active in governance matters. But institutional patterns vary considerably. A useful description of the range of faculty governance in different types of institutions[3] is provided by Baldridge and his colleagues (1978) and is worth summarizing here.

Private and public multiversities. "These institutions have strong faculties, and yet they are such complex organizations that they need strong administrators as well" (p. 89). Actually, many faculty members at these institutions avoid involvement in academic governance because the institutions are too complex and bewildering. The faculty has "enormous" influence over the academic departments, but "there is a high degree of fragmentation in these institutions, with the administrators carving out certain spheres of influence and the faculty carving out others." The observation of 89 percent of the presidents of Research Universities I and 80 percent of the presidents of Research Universities II that "most of the faculty members here are more interested in the affairs of their departments than they are in the governance of the entire institution" (Carnegie Council Surveys, 1978) is consistent with this characterization.

Elite liberal arts colleges were found by Baldridge and his associates to be closer than any other type of institutions to being purely collegial. The faculty and administration work closely together, and the faculty has a vested interest in certain institutionwide matters. The faculty is strong at both the departmental and academic senate levels. Again, the assessment of the presidents of such colleges responding to the Carnegie Council Surveys of 1978 tends to substantiate this view. Three-fourths of them indicate that "most" of their faculty members have an interest and concern in the governance of their institution. Nearly two-thirds of the presidents say that faculty interest in governance has increased since 1969-70.

---

[3]The classification of institutions used by Baldridge and others (1978) is similar to, but not identical with, that of the Carnegie Commission and Council. The comparisons I make between their findings and those of the Carnegie Surveys of 1978 must be regarded, therefore, as crude and tentative.

Public comprehensive institutions and public colleges are characterized as institutions in which the faculty has moderately strong departmental and senate organizations, but where "the outside influence of legislators and system-level controls is very strong . . . there are strong bureaucratic controls over the daily lives of the faculty" (Baldridge and others, 1978, pp. 92-93). The faculty in these institutions is usually inactive, and the administration exerts most of the influence over institution-wide activities. Although, as noted, the classification of institutions used by Baldridge and his associates differs significantly from that of the Carnegie Commission and Council, one can assume that many of the institutions in the Carnegie categories of Doctorate-granting Universities II and Comprehensive Universities and Colleges I and II fall within the category described. In the Council's surveys of 1978, between 40 and 50 percent of the presidents of these institutions say that most of the faculty members at their institutions have an interest and concern for academic governance, and between 60 and 67 percent of them say that the percentage of faculty members with such interests has increased.

Private liberal arts colleges are judged by Baldridge and his associates to have fairly weak faculties and strong administrations. The influence of the faculty is weakened not only by the power and authority of strong administrators, but also by environmental factors, such as the control of many of these colleges by religious denominations or by influences exerted by their surrounding communities. Institutionwide senates have been established only recently in these institutions. Again, the classification of institutions used for these observations differs from those of the Carnegie Commission and Council, and this difference may account for the fact that the presidents of Liberal Arts Colleges II—the most similar category in the Carnegie classification—do not perceive the interest of the members of their faculty in institutional matters to be that low. Almost one-half of them say that most of the faculty members at their institutions are more interested in the affairs of their departments than in governance of the entire institution, but 58 percent say most of their faculty do have an interest and concern in the governance of the institution (Carnegie Council Surveys, 1978).

Two-year colleges are regarded by Baldridge and his associates as "strongholds of administrative dominance. Faculty members here are the weakest in professional expertise, and environmental forces are the highest in all of higher education" (p. 94). Although these authors find faculty particupation in these colleges to be the lowest of any institutional group, more than one-half (51 percent) of the presidents of these institutions who responded to the Carnegie Council Surveys in 1978 say that most of their faculty have an interest and concern in the governance of the institution.

Overall, 58 percent of the presidents of American colleges and universities report that the general influence of faculty on campus policy and operations has increased since 1969. This increase should not, however, be interpreted to mean that the increased interest is expressed only through participation in the traditional faculty governance structures of the departments and senates. Some of it, at least, becomes apparent as a manifestation of the relatively recent introduction of faculty unionism.

Collective Bargaining

In 1969-70, 7.5 percent of all colleges and universities had collective bargaining contracts in force. By 1978, the proportion had tripled.

Thus far, faculty unionism is encountered mainly at public institutions—particularly at relatively new institutions and at institutions that provide no other alternative for faculty participation in institutional decision making. Two-year colleges, for example, reported both the greatest number of contracts with faculty unions in 1969 and the greatest gain in new contracts during the subsequent eight-year period (Carnegie Council Surveys, 1975).

On the whole, as the following responses to some of the pertinent propositions in collective bargaining suggest, faculty attitudes toward it tend to be positive.

Proposition	Percentage of faculty agreeing[a]	Percentage of faculty disagreeing[b]
Collective bargaining by faculty members has no place in a college or university	28%	72%
Collective bargaining by faculty is likely to bring higher salaries and improved benefits	77	23
Faculty members should be more militant in defending their interests	63	37
There are circumstances in which a strike would be a legitimate means of collective action by faculty members	62	38
Collective bargaining by faculty will tend to reduce student influence in academic decisions	35	65

[a]"Strongly agree" plus "agree with reservations."
[b]"Disagree with reservations" plus "strongly disagree."
Source: Carnegie Surveys, 1975.

Even at universities where strong faculty governments exist and where there is considerable hostility toward faculty bargaining, only 34 percent of the faculty agree that collective bargaining has no place in a college or university.

Despite faculty attitudes that are, on the whole, favorable to collective bargaining, I do not expect it to grow rapidly unless the day-to-day conditions of academic employment deteriorate badly under the pressures of enrollment decline and diminished financial resources. It has not yet penetrated deeply into the ranks of private institutions, which deal with bargaining units on an institution-by-institution basis rather than on a systemwide basis. Liberal arts colleges seem particularly resistant to the movement and in many ways, despite their small size, set the tone for much of higher education and evoke a special image of the academic man as collegial rather than confrontational in relationships with institutions. Of the presidents whose institutions do not now have agreements, about 17 percent report that they expect to have such agreements by 1983, but that would still leave more than two-thirds of all colleges and universities unaffected by the movement.

But conditions could change, and we can expect growing interest in collective bargaining if (1) faculty salaries, workloads, and working conditions are decided more frequently at a systemwide or statewide level than at a campus level; (2) part-time faculty members compete more extensively with full-time faculty members for teaching assignments; (3) state governments come to exert more coordinating control over private institutions; (4) interest and participation in the existing structures of academic governance decrease to the point that a majority of faculty members come to regard them as ineffective or as the tyranny of a minority; or (5) the powers exercised by presidents and other administrators in time of retrenchment come to be regarded by faculty members as oppressive or arbitrary.

Concluding Observations on the Academic Profession

College and university faculty members are members of split-level professions. Their skills and principles are drawn equally and simultaneously from their academic disciplines and their roles as educators. They recognize that there are ways to be a good historian or a good chemist, for example, and they spend many years acquiring knowledge in their fields. They know that there are also ways to be a good teacher and scholar, and their development in such activities is monitored closely by their colleagues. The professors' task is to balance and blend both of their callings effectively.

Some academics also develop a strong bond to the traditions and goals of their institutions. Such bonds are particularly close at those institutions where faculty members are deeply involved in decision making and come to regard themselves as agents of the institution's mission. They develop personal concerns for the effectiveness of higher learning, for the kind of educated men and women their institutions produce, and for the values that are honored in a college's daily life.

One of the consequences of the recent changes in higher education is that tensions are developing between the adherents of this professional academic tradition and the "marketplace" orientation of some colleges and universities. The trends that contribute most to create such tensions are:

1. *The increasing use of part-time faculty members,* particularly when such persons do not have the same qualifications for academic employment as those held by full-time, ladder-ranked faculty. One cannot honestly say that the problem derives from incompetence of part-time faculty members as such. In fact, there are certain situations in which part-time faculty members are superior. One obvious example is the teaching of esoteric languages or other subject specialties with which regular faculty members have imperfect familiarity. Another example involves the supervision of drills and other exercises designed to improve basic learning skills. Difficulties arise when the part-time and full-time faculty members are unequally knowledgeable and experienced in their fields but teach the same subjects in the same institutions. One frequently reported problem occurs in courses and programs designed for older students. Such instruction is frequently related to employment, and those who receive it express impatience with faculty members whose expertise is not as "practical" as they feel a need for. An anti-intellectual, anti-academic prejudice is often inferred from such incidents.

    Another difficulty is that part-time faculty members, while ineligible for some of the privileges of full-time academics, are also exempt from some of the responsibilities and obligations of full-time faculty. They are not really expected to have strong feelings of membership in the campus community and may, in fact, have divided institutional loyalties because they work for more than one college.

2. *The rapid growth of community colleges* has been made possible to a large extent by the contributions of faculty members whose preparation is quite different from that of the professoriate in four-year institutions. In 1975 about 18 percent of the total higher education faculty in the country were in two-year colleges and universities (Carnegie

Survey, 1975). Of that portion of the faculty, only 14 percent had doctorates (Cohen and Brawer, 1977, p. 119). It is at these institutions also that the tradition of academic self-governance is weakest. Questions about where this segment of the postsecondary teaching force really fits into the academic tradition could be regarded as peripheral when the number of two-year colleges was small, when many of them concentrated mainly on academic subjects, and when they were unevenly distributed across the country. But now they constitute a much larger segment of the institutional capacity of American higher education and serve more than one-third of all students enrolled.

3. *Increased opportunities for postsecondary education at institutions other than colleges and universities* tend to assign to traditional academics a more modest role than they once had in the total educational effort of the country. There has always been an enormous amount of education provided by churches, clubs, associations, libraries, museums, military installations, and in some of the workplaces of the nation. But instructors for such offerings were often regarded as amateurs by the professoriate on the campuses. What was new in the 1960s and 1970s is the professionalization of these faculties and the description of noncollegiate learning resources in terms that infer a generic relationship in kind and quality to the formal or traditional sources of learning represented by colleges and schools. The apparent effect of that depiction is to enhance the status of noncollegiate postsecondary education slightly at the expense of the status of the collegiate sector. And the professional relationship, if in fact there really needs to be one, between those who offer instruction in the two sectors becomes ambiguous.

4. *The deterioration* (however modest) *of the job market* in traditional institutions for men and women trained for teaching and research as professional academics may force some of these people into noncollegiate settings where their presence further blurs the distinctions between faculties in the two sectors.

5. *The advent of faculty collective bargaining* alters the re-
    lationship between academics and their institutions by
    making them less a part of the college or university's
    decision-making structure and more a part of an adver-
    sarial manpower force that the college or university
    must reckon with.

Some of the tensions between the professional academic
tradition and the emerging forces of the educational labor
market were just becoming obvious as the 1970s ended. It may
be that they need not be resolved in the 1980s—or, for that
matter, ever. Eventually it may be found that the clienteles of
the two sectors are sufficiently distinctive, and the educational
programs sufficiently discrete, that specialized faculties will be
required for each. Alternatively, professional academics may
someday accept their noncollegiate colleagues as peers. But I
do not regard that as a likely possibility soon. In fact, I expect
the tensions between the professional academic tradition and
other educational enterprises to be increasingly important
parts of academic life for many years into the future.

4

The Presidents and
the Trustees

The initiative for creating the earliest American colleges and universities came from private citizens who recognized the country's need for the education such institutions could provide. They organized themselves to generate public interest and financial support for the colleges that were to be founded and to provide overall direction and policy guidance for the new educational enterprises. Later, when the states created public institutions of higher learning, provision was made for the appointment or election of persons to assume responsibility for their direction and policy. In both cases, the persons designated as responsible for the public trust in American colleges and universities—the trustees—can be described as corporate leadership for higher education. In the sense that their authority derives from the public, rather than from internal election and support, it might also be said that they exert external leadership. Internal leadership was and still is provided by the men and women the trustees select to be college and university presidents with responsibilities for day-to-day management.

The Trustees

There are about 47,000 trustees and regents in the United States, and they serve on more than 2,300 boards governing more than 3,000 campuses (Magarell, 1977). In general, they are expected to: exercise such oversight and direction as may be necessary to make sure that the purposes of the institution as perceived by the founders and defined by the purposes of its endowment are properly served; initiate or approve major changes in the institution's mission as they become necessary or desirable; monitor the use of institutional resources; seek out financial support when it is needed; advise the internal leadership of the institution on matters of policy; and appoint and dismiss the institution's presidents. Boards of trustees are also expected to provide a bridge (some observers would say "buffer") between society and the institution and serve as a "court of last resort" for the resolution of internal conflicts within the institution (see Perkins, 1973, p. 203).

But these guidelines are broad, and a lot of room is left for interpretation. For example, of the 599 chairmen of boards of trustees at the 1974 meeting of the Association of Governing Boards of Colleges and Universities, 85 percent agreed that "trustees have legitimate prerogatives in educational and curriculum areas," and 82 percent agreed that trustees and administrators should be concerned with the equitable determination of faculty workloads (Corson, 1977, pp. 3-5). It has also been suggested that trustees should examine the student demographics to see whether admissions and financial aid policies are "appropriate," seek more information about faculty recruitment and evaluations of faculty members who are under consideration for promotion, and seek evidence of the achievement of the institution's graduates in order to see how well it is performing. I am certain that, on most campuses, the faculty and administration would state that such actions are more appropriately taken by the internal leadership.

Trustees of private institutions usually serve for stipulated terms and, by filling vacancies on the board, choose their own successors. Trustees of public institutions may be appointed by a governor, appointed by a governor and confirmed by the legislature or some other official body, elected in statewide elections (or in district elections in the case of two-year institutions), or elected by state legislatures (Paltridge, Hurst, and Morgan, 1973, p. 19). There are variations on all of these methods, and the charters of many institutions also provide that certain state or university officials be members of the board.

Information made available by the Association of Governing Boards makes possible the following summary of the characteristics of the men and women who become members of boards of trustees at American colleges and universities: Approximately 85 percent of them are male; two-thirds are 50 years old or older; and about 10 percent are under 40; 90 percent have baccalaureate degrees, and 32 percent have professional or doctorate degrees. About one-third of all trustees hold an administrative or executive position in business or industry; approximately one-fourth are engaged in the professions, and one in seven is involved in education as an administrator, teacher, or college student (Corson, 1977).

During the 1960s and early 1970s, there was a tendency for colleges and universities to add faculty and student representatives to the boards of trustees in response to demands that the governance of higher education become more "democratic" and provide for the participation of all groups of people who are involved in it in any major way. However, in its report, *Governance of Higher Education,* the Carnegie Commission on Higher Education (1973c) opposed both faculty and student representation on the governing boards of colleges and universities where they were employed or enrolled. The rationale for this position was that such membership would constitute a potential conflict of interest. In any case, a few faculty members and students cannot really be representative of the full diversity of their constituencies.

As a matter of fact, a case could be made for the proposition that the only special interests of any kind that should be guaranteed representation on the board of a college or university are those of the institution's founders. Members of a religious denomination might, for example, expect the interests of their church to be given consideration in the policies and programs of the institutions they create and support. But institutions that are intended to serve the objectives of the general public probably do not need trustees who hold any qualifications other than that they are "intelligent persons with sensitive appreciation of the values" of the institution (Thompson, 1972, p. 167). Efforts to stipulate that certain seats on a board should be reserved for officers of state or local governments; for alumni of the institution; for members of ethnic groups; for persons who represent labor, or business, or the professions; or for student and faculty representatives alter the emphasis on service to all to an emphasis on compromise in the interests of certain groups. A carefully selected board of trustees can include men and women of many different interests and accomplishments, even if places on the board are not specifically reserved for representatives of different viewpoints. Moreover, advice on technical matters or issues in which certain groups have a stake can be sought much more effectively from ad hoc special purpose committees or from informal consultation with individuals than from formal representatives on a board.

One source of difficulties in some state institutions is the appointment of trustees or regents by a governor. Such appointments are often regarded as political plums awarded to pay off political debts. To overcome this difficulty, it has been recommended by many, including the Carnegie Commission on Higher Education, that such appointments be made subject to senatorial or other legislative confirmation.

In the 1960s I had occasion to study the careers and qualifications of all of the regents of the University of California that had served between 1868 and 1968. I had the following general reaction:

- On the whole, the University of California has been fortunate in attracting to its service men and women of considerable distinction and influence in the state.

- The political allegiances of many regents were put aside as their service on the board lengthened. Many regents remained on the board long after the governors that appointed them left office. On matters concerning the university, several eventually became outspoken opponents of the governors that appointed them.

- The strongest regents were appointed regents. The weakest (with one or two exceptions) were ex-officio regents of all kinds. Particularly weak were lieutenant governors, speakers of the state assembly, and alumni representatives.

• Many regents became profoundly loyal to the University of California, giving it not only their time and their money, but also deep affection. Among them were some of the institutions' most vigorous defenders in times of political attack and fiscal stringencies.

In their report on changes in university organization, E. Gross and P. Grambsch (1974) asked administrators and faculty members at 68 universities to rank the most powerful constituencies at their institution. In 1964 and again in 1971, the trustees or regents ranked above federal and state governments, students, faculty, alumni, parents, private citizens, and administrators (Table 18) as most powerful. Only the presidents

Table 18. The overall power structure of American universities, 1964 and 1971

	Rank	
Power holder	1964	1971
President	1	1
Regents or trustees	2	2
Vice presidents	3	3
Deans of professional schools	4	4
Deans of liberal arts schools	5	6
Deans of graduate schools	6	5
Faculty	7	7
Legislators	8	9
Chairmen	9	8
Federal government	10	10
State government	11	11
Students	12	14
Grants	13	12
Alumni	14	13
Citizens	15	15
Partners	16	16

Source: Gross and Grambsch, 1974, p. 122.

of the institutions in the study were accorded higher ranking. In 1978, asked about the increase or decrease of power of various constituencies since 1969-70, 49.6 percent of the college and university presidents say that the power of the governing boards has increased; 59 percent say that the power of the organized faculty has increased; and 55 percent say that administrators other than presidents have acquired more influence. In the Carnegie Council site visits, we explored this matter more fully and found little change since 1971. In the site visit ranking, governing boards rank fourth in a field of eight groups that included administrators other than presidents, individual faculty members, organized faculty members, departments, student government, and individual students. The highest ranking is given the presidents themselves.

The Presidents

On college and university campuses, the broadest perspectives for viewing the general health and prospects of individual institutions are those of the presidents. They have access to considerable amounts of information—some of which is privileged and confidential—concerning the operations of their institutions. It is also part of their job to be well-informed on external developments that may affect the institutions they lead. Most of them come to their positions with 25 to 30 years prior experience in higher education. Eighty-five percent of the presidents of four-year institutions and 89 percent of the presidents of two-year institutions hold Ph.D.'s or Ed.D.'s (Table 19). All but a few have, at one time or another, been members of a college faculty. Most of them have also served as department chairmen, deans, or vice presidents before being appointed to a presidency. About 20 percent of them were presidents at other institutions before assuming their current positions.

Length of Service

One sobering thought for would-be reformers of colleges and universities is that the presidents they enlist in their cause today may have relatively little time in office to help them implement their proposals. Across the country, there were, on the average, 359 turnovers in college presidencies each year between 1974-75 and 1977-78—a turnover rate of about 13 percent a year (Table 20). This helps to explain why about 13 percent of the presidents in 1978 had been in office a year or less, and why more than one-half of the presidents in office in 1978

Table 19. Presidents' highest degree earned, by Carnegie classification, in percentages, 1978

Highest degree earned	Research Universities		Doctorate-granting Institutions		Comprehensive Colleges and Universities		Liberal Arts Colleges		Two-Year Colleges	Average percentage, all institutions
	I	II	I	II	I	II	I	II		
Ph.D.	80%	92%	75%	83%	64%	76%	67%	75%	41%	69%
Ed.D.		8	8	17	11	12		8	48	16
LL.D./J.D./D.B.A./M.D.	20		8		14	8	13			6
Th.D./D.D.						4	6	17		2
M.A./M.S./M.B.A.	8		8		7		6		7	4
B.A./B.S.					4		6		4	2
N	10	12	12	6	28	25	15	12	27	

Source: Special study of presidents of 147 institutions made by the Carnegie Council staff, 1978.

Table 20. Turnover in the presidencies of colleges and universities, 1974-75 to 1977-78

			Rate of turnover (percentage)								
			All institutions			Public institutions			Private institutions		
	Turnovers	Total number of presidents	Total	Four-year	Two-year	Total	Four-year	Two-year	Total	Four-year	Two-year
1974-75	352	3,038	11.8%	n.a.	n.a.	n.a.	n.a.	n.a.	n.a.	n.a.	n.a.
1975-76	399	3,055	13.2	13.6%	12.6%	12.6%	13.9%	11.8%	13.8%	13.5%	15.5%
1976-77	362	3,075	12.0	12.6	10.8	10.8	10.8	10.8	13.0	13.4	10.6
1977-78	324	2,467	13.1	12.7	10.2	13.2	13.0	13.9	9.9	11.7	8.6

Source: National Center for Education Statistics, *Education Directory*, 1975, 1976, 1977, 1978.

Table 21. Average length of years in office of incumbent presidents of colleges and universities in 1978 and their immediate predecessors, by Carnegie classification

	Research Universities		Doctorate-granting Institutions		Comprehensive Colleges and Universities		Liberal Arts Colleges		Two-Year Colleges
	I	II	I	II	I	II	I	II	
Mean									
Incumbents	6.0	5.3	5.2	5.9	6.5	6.1	6.7	5.7	6.9
Predecessors	9.7	7.5	9.0	8.7	11.3	9.2	10.9	9.2	7.2
Median									
Incumbents	6.0	4.0	4.0	4.0	5.5	4.0	6.3	4.0	5.9
Predecessors	7.0	5.5	6.5	6.0	9.5	5.5	9.5	7.0	5.5

Source: Carnegie Council Surveys, 1978.

were appointed after 1972 (Table 21). And, unless they exceed the average (mean) term in office of their predecessors (8.8 years), the presidents who were appointed in 1978 may be out of office (at least at their present institutions) by 1986 or 1987 (Table 22).

Some reasons for presidential turnover have to do with their age. Of 147 presidents studied by the Council's staff, the

Table 22. Years of service of college and university
presidents in 1978 and their predecessors

Presidents in 1978		*Immediate predecessors of presidents in 1978*	
Number	Years served	Number	Years served
322	1 or less[a]	108	1 or less[a]
219	2	200	2
239	3	185	3
214	4	181	4
159	5	145	5
198	6	123	6
219	7	137	7
162	8	119	8
112	9	109	9
132	10	105	10
97	11	45	11
44	12	75	12
98	13	35	13
50	14	31	14
28	15	58	15
123	16 or more[b]	44	16
2,416		61	17
		39	18
Median 5.3 years		28	19
Mean 6.4 years		32	20
		30	21
		17	22
		19	23
		10	24
		30	25
		56	26 or more[c]
		2,024	
		Median 6.5 years	
		Mean 8.8 years	

[a]Counted 1 for purposes of averaging.
[b]Counted 16 for purposes of averaging.
[c]Counted 26 for purposes of averaging.
Source: Carnegie Council Surveys, 1978.

age range was from 35 to 69, and the mean age was 54.3 (Table 23). Presidents who have reached the average age can anticipate only 10 to 15 additional years before retirement, and some may choose to retire early.

Table 23. Average age of presidents by Carnegie classification, 1978

	Average age		
Research Universities I	54.0		
Research Universities II	57.0		
Doctorate-granting Institutions I	51.0		
Doctorate-granting Institutions II	59.0		
Comprehensive Colleges and Universities I	56.0	*MEAN*	*54.3 years*
Comprehensive Colleges and Universities II	56.0		
Liberal Arts Colleges I	55.0		
Liberal Arts Colleges II	50.5		
Two-Year Colleges	50.5		

Source: Special study of presidents of 147 institutions by Carnegie Council staff, 1978.

The longest periods of service as president, both for incumbents and their predecessors, are found in the Comprehensive Colleges and Universities I, Liberal Arts Colleges I, and Research Universities I (Table 21). Why this is so can be explained only in terms of assumptions about the reasons presidents leave office, and about the governance and other characteristics of the institutions they lead. One observation is that student disruption of operations has not been a significant factor in the resignation or dismissal of college presidents for several years. Natural retirement, death in office, or controversies involving faculties, trustees, and authorities outside the institutions are more commonly the cause of vacancies. Presidential relationships with the faculty are especially crucial; in several instances, faculty votes of "no-confidence" have triggered dismissals.

Comprehensive Colleges and Universities I, where conditions for presidential survival appear to be especially strong, are relatively large, have at least 2,000 students, and appear to be growing. When asked what major changes on their campuses had a beneficial effect in the past 10 years, presidents on these campuses frequently mention new buildings, new programs, the addition of professional schools, and efforts to reach out to new clienteles. Seven percent of them mention that they received more state support than in earlier years (Carnegie Council Surveys, 1978). Such conditions augur well for college presidents.

Another factor in the long tenure of presidents of Comprehensive Colleges and Universities I is that, of all types of four-year institutions, these have the longest experience with faculty collective bargaining—7 percent of them had collective bargaining in 1969-70, and 22 percent have it now (Carnegie Council Surveys, 1978). Although some presidents regard collective bargaining as a negative factor in the life of their institutions during the past 10 years, a few mention it favorably. One hypothesis is that collective bargaining contracts codify as well as restrict the authority exercised by college and university presidents. They reduce the number of ad hoc decisions that need to be made by presidents and their subordinates, particularly in sensitive personnel areas that could engender disharmony with the faculty. Moreover, collective bargaining gives faculty members procedures short of seeking the dismissal of a president for dealing with their dissatisfactions.

Finally, as institutions of higher education become more complex, the kinds of decisions reserved to presidents have an increasingly higher order of generality. Many of the petty and distasteful decisions that have to be made by presidents at small colleges can be made at large institutions by deans and department chairmen. Departmental appeals to presidential authority at large institutions may imply indecision or weakness at lower levels and are usually made only as a last resort. Another feature of such institutions is that the internal units operate independently. In institutions with high degrees of internal departmental and divisional autonomy, the interaction of presidents with individual faculty members and students is infrequent; these presidents are insulated from internal sources of conflict and dissent, leaving only governing boards and, in the case of public institutions, external governmental authority as potential sources of challenge.

Liberal Arts Colleges I and Research Universities I, in different ways, also insulate presidents from internal conflicts by giving considerable autonomy to the faculty and internal departments and divisions. In addition, these colleges and universities are some of the most prestigious institutions in the country and, therefore, attract well-known, highly skilled leaders who have a built-in edge on survival in office in their own considerable intellectual and managerial abilities.

Presidential Authority

In the Carnegie Council's survey of college and university presidents in 1978, an effort was made to assess their estimates of their own authority within their institutions. First, they were asked if they had authority commensurate with the demands of their jobs and then, if their authority had increased since 1969. The results of this part of the survey are summarized in Table 24. In both Comprehensive Colleges and Universities I and Research Universities I, more than 70 percent of the presidents say they have authority commensurate with their jobs, but even higher percentages of presidents in other types of institutions give the same answer. One factor in this difference is the increasing role played by external agencies, particularly state coordinating agencies and the federal agencies, in college and university matters. These governmental involvements increase a president's accountability to external authorities and are viewed as eroding his or her own internal authority. Because the governmental presence is most evident in large public institutions, it is not surprising that it is not regarded as having a serious influence in Liberal Arts Colleges II.

Liberal Arts Colleges II, as a matter of fact, are characterized by long traditions of relatively powerful presidents. Their small faculties are not broken down into autonomous departments and divisions, and in times of financial stringency, which many colleges are now experiencing, institutions like these tend to give their presidents even more authority than they have in normal times. Fifty-six percent of the presidents of these institutions say their authority has increased since 1969 (Table 24).

Table 24. Presidential perceptions of their authority, by Carnegie classification, 1978

	Research Universities		Doctorate-granting Institutions		Comprehensive Colleges and Universities		Liberal Arts Colleges		Two-Year Colleges
	I	II	I	II	I	II	I	II	
Percentage who "strongly agree" or "agree with reservations" that "the president of this institution has authority commensurate with the demands of the job"	71%	85%	64%	88%	76%	85%	83%	94%	94%
Percentage who "strongly agree" or "agree with reservations" that "the authority of the president of this institution has increased since 1969"	34	26	21	25	44	34	21	56	43

Source: Carnegie Council Surveys, 1978.

The strong chief administrator tradition also prevails at two-year colleges. Some of these institutions are quite large, but their departments and other academic divisions exist largely at the pleasure of the presidents, and most major decisions are made by administrative committees. Two-year college presidents also are likely to draw their strength more from their relationships with the surrounding communities (from which their own boards of trustees may be chosen) than from those they may cultivate on the campuses. Although these institutions have been unionized to a considerable extent, the impacts of faculty bargaining on presidential authority either are not yet clear or are judged by the presidents to be benign.

Presidential Concerns in 1978

They say it in many ways: "a chronic funding gap," "static or shrinking resource base," "costs cut to the bone," "inflation," "cash flow," and "$." However it is said, it means *financing* and is the most frequent response of presidents in 1978 when we asked them: "Of all of the problems confronting your institution right now, which one is of the greatest concern to you?" In all, more than 1,000 presidents, 45 percent of our respondents, answer "financing" (Table 25), outnumbering those who mention the second-ranking concern—decreasing enrollments—almost three to one.

Presidential concern with money is hardly new. After all, the financial health of a president's college or university is high on the list of his or her responsibilities. When H. Hodgkinson asked a similar question in 1969, the responses of about 75 percent of the presidents "clustered magnificently around the problem of getting adequate funding to keep the program going" (Hodgkinson, 1971, p. 25).

Financial problems are almost certainly of greater concern to presidents than their direct response to the word *financing* indicates. Such problems are, in fact, implicit in other responses to the survey. For example, "decreasing enrollments," the second most frequently given response to our question about current presidential concerns, may be equated with

Table 25. Frequency and percentage of presidents responding in 1978 to the question
"Of all of the problems confronting your institution right now, which one is of the greatest concern to you?"

Of greatest concern	Presidents, public institutions	Presidents, private institutions	Presidents, all institutions	Percentage of all presidents
Financing	432	592	1,024	45%
Decreasing enrollments	151	230	381	17
Improving quality of education	205	82	287	13
Governmental regulation and coordination	163	7	170	7
Need for physical facilities	79	7	86	4
Collective bargaining	79	0	79	3
Public confidence	28	4	32	1
Increasing enrollments	19	12	31	1
Recruiting students	27	2	29	1
Other	84	91	175	8
Total	1,267	1,027	2,294	

Source: Carnegie Council Surveys, 1978.

decreased tuition revenues. And "inflation," originally tabulated separately in our study, was mentioned by 64 presidents. The "inflation" response is included under the general heading of "financing" in Table 25, however, because it is not clear that the responding presidents intended to make a sharp distinction between high costs and low revenues as financing difficulties.

When the responses of the presidents are broken down according to the Carnegie classification of institutions, the highest percentage (75) that perceives financing as their greatest concern is found in Doctorate-granting Institutions II (Table 26). This may be because these institutions, to a greater extent than other universities, rely heavily on undergraduate tuition and enrollment-based government funding formulas to support high-cost graduate and professional instruction and research. The possibility that high costs are a particular concern of the presidents of these institutions is strongly suggested by the fact that 24 percent of them cited "inflation" as their greatest concern. In fact, presidents of these institutions comprise one-third of all presidents who mentioned inflation in that context.

The concern for financing shown by presidents of comprehensive and two-year colleges is below the average for all presidents, no doubt reflecting the dominance of public institutions in these categories.

The financial problems of Liberal Arts Colleges II are related to the diseconomies of their size (many have less than 1,000 students); the limits of their pricing structure because of competition with low-cost public institutions with more comprehensive offerings; their small endowments; and their limited sources of nontuition revenues.

The fact that more than one-third of the presidents of Liberal Arts Colleges I rank "decreasing enrollments" as the problem of greatest concern to them was not anticipated except, perhaps, as has already been suggested, as the major cause of their financing problems. It is also surprising that, although decreasing enrollments hold second rank among problems of greatest concern to presidents right now, the proportion of presidents ranking it "first" is not higher than it is. The coming decline in the nation's college-age population

Table 26. Percentage of presidents responding in 1978 to the question: "Of all of the problems confronting your institution right now, which one is of the greatest concern to you?" by Carnegie classification

Of greatest concern	Research Universities		Doctorate-granting Institutions		Comprehensive Colleges and Universities		Liberal Arts Colleges		Two-Year Colleges
	I	II	I	II	I	II	I	II	
Financing	62%	48%	57%	75%	40%	45%	39%	58%	39%
Decreasing enrollments	3	4	5	7	14	18	39	23	14
Improving quality of education	0	3	0	0	16	17	16	8	14
Governmental regulation and coordination	18	9	10	4	8	6	0	1	11
Need for physical facilities	3	3	0	0	5	3	0	0	6
Collective bargaining	3	6	3	11	5	3	0	0	5
Public confidence	0	0	5	0	1	2	0	0	2
Increasing enrollments	0	0	3	0	3	3	2	0	1
Recruiting students	0	3	3	0	1	0	0	0	2
Other	11	24	15	4	9	3	5	10	6

Source: Carnegie Council Surveys, 1978.

has been well publicized for most of the past decade, and one would expect presidents to be more concerned about it than our survey results indicate. Following are some of the reasons why they are not concerned.

- The decreases are not yet a reality on many campuses. In fact, in 31 institutions in our survey, enrollment not only was still increasing in 1978, but presidents of these institutions rank "increasing enrollment" as their greatest problem.
- Some presidents have strategies in reserve for reaching out to new sources of students.
- Some presidents believe their institutions can survive comfortably with whatever share of the decreases may occur there.
- Some presidents hold the optimistic view that, whatever happens, the worst will affect other institutions and not their own—"it can't happen here."

In any event, of the presidents who see declining enrollments as their greatest problem, almost twice as many are in private institutions as are in public ones.

"Improving the quality of education" is the third-ranking concern of the presidents in our survey. But those who give educational quality top importance cluster in two types of institutions:

- Liberal Arts Colleges I, which include many elite institutions and in which enrollment decreases are feared by a substantial number of presidents
- Comprehensive Colleges and Universities, Liberal Arts Colleges II, and Two-Year Colleges, where open admissions policies are likely to prevail.

Concerns for governmental regulation and coordination and needs for new physical facilities are found most frequently among presidents of public institutions.

Concluding Observations

The distinction between the types of leadership given by trustees and presidents has never been as clear as it might be. Presidents are frequently called upon to make decisions and take action without the advice and consent of the trustees. They are, after all, on the scene when decisions have to be made and when calling trustees together for deliberation and guidance is not always possible. For their part, trustees are often tempted to overprotect their policy decisions by engaging in detailed direction of a college's affairs. In times of difficulty, however, trustees appear willing to give presidents considerable authority, and it is in this context that the strength and authority presidents feel they have at the beginning of the 1980s probably should be viewed.

In its final report, the Carnegie Council on Policy Studies in Higher Education (1980) suggested that boards of trustees concentrate more on searching for leaders than, as they seem to have been doing of late, survival managers. The Council observed that "the challenges of the future require leadership. The day-to-day management can be supplied at the vice-presidential level."

The Council also suggested the adoption of procedures for an early informal review of a president (say after 2 years) with the understanding that following such a review the total term of office will be about 10 years in the absence of strong reasons to the contrary. I am personally attracted to the idea of informal reviews not only after two years, but every five years thereafter. The objective of assuring a president that he or she will be given enough time to make significant contributions to an institution's destiny is sound, and 10 years seems to me to be about right as an average target. However, opportunities for excellent presidents to serve for even longer periods of time should not be limited. There is also much to be said for relatively frequent reviews as a means of monitoring the stamina and vitality of an administration and providing convenient, nonpejorative occasions for colleges and their presidents to consider the need for a leadership change.

The final suggestion of the Council on this matter is that governing boards of colleges and universities be determined to stand behind presidents who do well. When one stops to think about that, it seems too bad that the point need be made at all.

The view that trustees exist only to pick and fire presidents is cynical and short-sighted. The responsibilities of trustees go beyond that. They really should be official links between the institution and society beyond it. They should be viewed as sources of information about the needs of their communities and the directions of social and economic movement that may affect the institution. And they should know enough and care enough about the institutions entrusted to their oversight that they can and will protect them from unreasonable and dangerous public clamoring of all sorts. It is this role that all too often is given short shrift in decisions to appoint people to college boards of trustees. This is also the role that presidents of institutions often fail to appreciate. I remember an occasion when, at a meeting attended mostly by college presidents, the time came to ask how the ideas that had been agreed upon could be disseminated to the public. I was dismayed to find that a suggestion that the college trustees be enlisted in the cause was considered out of the question and naive, yet there was considerable enthusiasm for working with local service clubs. It seemed tragic to me that what should be the natural links — between institutions and the society around them were avoided in favor of those that involved more direct relations between presidents and community leaders.

It may well be, unhappily, that in the difficult years ahead the first fence to be mended at some institutions may be the one between the internally oriented and externally oriented leadership in higher education.

Part Two

Institutional Change

The title of the final report of the Carnegie Council on Policy Studies in Higher Education is *Three Thousand Futures: The Next Twenty Years for Higher Education.* It was chosen to reflect the fact that each of our country's colleges and universities has its own future, and that general trends and prevailing practices do not affect all institutions in the same ways.

This theme is repeated in the following chapters, where I consider the concept of diversity in higher education and the ways in which colleges and universities are adapting to falling enrollments and reduced resources.

I do not, however, discuss in detail one general trend—the tendency of institutions to emulate the most prestigious, largest, and most secure colleges and universities. The most frequently mentioned model, of course, is Harvard University, which began as a small college and became a major research university. The fact that Harvard's evolution took more than 300 years and was favored by a number of historical circumstances we may not see again does not deter the leaders of some colleges today from believing that a similar destiny awaits their own institutions.

The impulse of colleges and universities to emulate prestigious institutions is one reason some observers fear for the future of diversity in American higher education. It also explains why much that is written about higher education takes the university model for granted as a norm rather than as one end of a spectrum. It should take nothing away from the achievements of major universities, however, to say that the proposition that all institutions of higher education want to be like them is overdrawn. Many colleges, in fact, are satisfied to be just what they are. Some would rather be a Swarthmore, an Oberlin, or a Reed than a Harvard. And the pull of many two-year institutions (and some four-year institutions) in the 1970s appeared to be in directions quite different from those followed by traditional colleges and universities.

The prevailing direction of change in the 1970s was not toward university status per se. It was, instead toward comprehensiveness. If one subscribes to David Riesman's metaphor of the snake that represents institutions of higher education extending from the head, where prestigious universities are found, to the tail, where the least comprehensive institutions are, the comprehensive universities and colleges must be seen as forming a very long, bulky midsection. This midsection is big, because it includes four-year institutions created by the states and 239 private institutions with similar characteristics (Carnegie Council, 1980). The midsection is likely to get even longer and bulkier in coming decades, because it is the natural resting place for those institutions that do strive to become a part of the snake's neck or head but have not yet made it. Nearer the tail, the midsection is also likely to absorb small, doctorate-granting universities that encounter troubles in the 1980s, two-year colleges and liberal arts colleges that reach out to new clienteles and establish new programs at the subdoctoral level, and many small colleges that merge with existing comprehensive institutions. It may be reduced slightly by those comprehensive institutions that acquire university status, but that reduction will be small—only 13 university have been established since 1940, and only 41 of the universities that existed in 1976 had been some other kind of institution six years earlier.

As the ensuing chapters will make clear, the move toward comprehensiveness may not have resulted from status-seeking as much as it has from the responses of colleges and universities to the decrease of their traditional sources of enrollments and to opportunities to render new types of services to new types of learners.

5

Diversity in
Higher Education

In older societies, the expected products of education were well-schooled members of an aristocracy or of a few professions; their colleges tended to be somewhat alike. In modern, open, and democratic societies such as our own, the expected products of education may be quite varied, and higher education is highly diversified.

Diversity's Many Forms

Literally, diversity is a condition of having differences, and in higher education it characterizes any system in which individual institutions or groups of institutions differ from one another in any way. But that definition applies to several, often overlapping types of diversity. It can be programmatic, procedural, systemic, constituental, or reputational—to suggest only a few of its forms.

Programmatic diversity involves the comprehensiveness of the curriculum of an institution. Procedural diversity develops less from what is taught than from how it is taught; less from what is done than from how it is done. Systemic diversity is found among institutions of different types (for example, research universities or liberal arts colleges), sizes, and control (public, private, religious, nonsectarian). Constituent diversity results from differences in the family backgrounds, abilities, preparation, values, and educational goals of students. There are also differences in institutional prestige and forms of internal governance.

It is especially useful to distinguish between *internal* and *external* diversity. Internal diversity results when institutions seek to serve more than one goal or mission, to provide education for special groups within their constituencies, or to utilize more than one approach or technique to achieve their educational objectives. One rich source of internal diversity is the variety of subjects that are taught. It is also made possible by the provision of alternative teaching and learning conditions and by the existence of options in the use of instructional technology. It may also result from the work of special colleges or other discrete programs within an institution.

External diversity, also often called *institutional* diversity, involves differentiation *among* colleges and universities. It may be associated with such factors as location, particular personnel and students, or a particular physical plant and environment. It may be structural and programmatic. It can involve types of control, special constituencies, institutional missions, or levels of selectivy of admissions requirements.

Diversity is not always beneficial. It often frustrates efforts to establish uniform standards for educational achievement. It accentuates differences among people to such an extent that common values and ethical practices may be difficult to teach and sustain. And programs and procedures that are adopted only because they are novel are usually frivolous and wasteful.

Nevertheless, diversity is prized in American higher education because it recognizes differences in people. It also:

- Increases the range of choices available to learners
- Makes higher education available to virtually everyone, despite differences among individuals
- Matches education to the needs, goals, learning styles, speed, and abilities of individual students
- Enables institutions to select their own missions and confine their activities to those that are consistent with their location, resources, levels of instruction, and clienteles
- Responds to the pressures of a society that is itself characterized by great complexity and diversity

●   Becomes a precondition of college and university freedom and autonomy because the greater the differences are among institutions, the more difficult it is for a central authority to convert them into instruments of indoctrination rather than of education.

What's Happening to Diversity Among Institutions?

The character of diversity in American higher education is constantly shifting. But it will never disappear entirely. After all, the dimensions of diversity are, in the long run, determined not only by colleges and universities, but also by whatever one might call the total "system" or "resources" of higher learning. For example, an enormous amount of diversity of educational endeavor is provided by proprietary institutions, museums, private industry, and military establishments. Moreover, as institutions become more comprehensive, as they merge with one another, and as they add functions and programs, they become internally more diverse even though diversity among institutions may be diminished.

It is also clear that developments that constrain diversity of one kind may have a countervailing positive effect on diversity of another kind. As may be seen from the matching of constraints and inducements below, the issues of diversity are seldom clear-cut.

Constraints	*Inducements*
Declining enrollments generate fewer demands from students.	Declining enrollments stimulate efforts to attract new kinds of students with new programs.
Increasing the size of institutions diverts enrollments from small colleges, forces them to close, and thereby decreases diversity among institutions.	Large institutions tend to diversify internally, creating many virtually independent schools, centers, branch campuses, or even large departments. For some pur-

Constraints	*Inducements*
	poses, e.g., integration of racial groups, internal diversification is better than diversity among institutions.
Highly trained faculty who hold degrees from doctorate-granting and research institutions exert pressures to transform liberal arts and comprehensive college in the image of their graduate alma maters. This possibility is particularly great when there is a national over-supply of Ph.D.'s, and top quality teachers can be recruited at institutions where they would not be found years ago.	In times when there is an abundance of faculty talent, fewer personnel restraints exist to thwart efforts to establish new programs.
Fiscal austerity results in institutional closures and mergers and reduced programming.	Some new programs are started in times of fiscal austerity as a means of attracting new students and new support. Mergers that occur in such times merely convert some of the diversity *among* institutions into diversity *within* institutions.
The sudden popularity of certain missions, e.g., vocational education, tends to dominate higher education.	Some institutions adapt to new missions by adding new programs.

Constraints	*Inducements*
New technologies tend to standardize instruction and administrative procedures.	New technologies make it possible for institutions to conduct programs in areas that lie beyond the capabilities of existing talent and resources.

None of that is to say, however, that there are no threats to diversity in American higher education. They do exist and take several forms. Among them are the demise of some institutions, centralized state or agency coordination of higher education, collective bargaining, public acceptance of college and university stereotypes, and overzealous regulation.

The effects on diversity of institutions that close are too obvious to elaborate. And, unhappily, as we will observe in later chapters, it is precisely the kind of institution that strives most for distinctiveness that is most vulnerable to failure. It might be noted also that the survival strategy of some institutions may, in fact, be to change their missions and become less distinctive so that they can appeal to a larger clientele. No one can blame them for adopting this survival strategy. But their decision nevertheless has the effect of diminishing diversity—almost as though they closed down.

Centralized state coordination of higher education and the increase in the number of multicampus institutions may also threaten diversity. This is ironic because some of the first multicampus systems were planned as a means of fostering different missions and programs within a single institution. In practice, however, the centralized administration of large systems of higher education often involves standardization and regulation. Excessive controls over such matters as course number and descriptions, student-faculty ratios, admissions requirements, and faculty workloads inevitably tend toward sameness rather than distinctiveness.

Faculty collective bargaining may impair diversity when it binds institutions to agreements on workload and other working conditions that are based on regional or systemwide union practices and demands rather than on the missions of individual institutions.

Standardization and regulation that are imposed, often inadvertently, by nongovernmental agencies, such as regional or professional accrediting associations, also can be a threat to diversity if they are too rigid, too detailed, and enforced without sensitivity to the unique values and functions each institution wishes to serve. Restrictions on diversity may also take the form of the definitions used to determine the eligibility of certain types of institutions (public or private, religious or secular) for federal, state, or even philanthropic financial assistance.

More subtly than regulation, the public perception of what a college or university ought to be can also threaten diversity. When most of the country's college graduates were alumni of small liberal arts colleges, public conceptions of the proper or common collegiate experience were influenced by the models provided by those kinds of institutions. The model was reinforced by the "collegiate" movies of the 1940s and 1950s. This stereotype is now changing as the lion's share of college graduates are products of public comprehensive institutions.

Diversity is not really threatened, but its virtues are certainly neutralized when institutions fail to make their distinctiveness known. If students are to genuinely benefit from diversity, they need to know before they enroll in an institution that all colleges and universities are not alike. Good academic counseling is a friend to diversity, as well as to the students who benefit from it. Unfortunately, American higher education, which is more diversified than that of any other country in the world, so far has an undistinguished record in providing students with good information and counseling services.

In his study of *Institutions in Transition* for the Carnegie Commission on Higher Education, Hodgkinson (1971) found that "institutions of higher learning are becoming more like each other than was true in the past." In fact, he said "Often one finds two institutions within a mile or so of each other, so much alike they could have been stamped out of the same cookie cutter" (p. 277). His findings are reviewed and updated in the following observations:

1. Hodgkinson found that the college experience of students increasingly occurs in public institutions. As may be seen in Figures 3 and 4, both the number of private institutions and their proportion of enrollments have continued to decline. In fact, in 1977 more than three out of every four students were in public institutions. This trend is particularly disturbing because private colleges are important sources of diversity.

Figure 3. Private institutions as a percentage of all U.S. institutions of higher education, 1955, 1965, and 1977

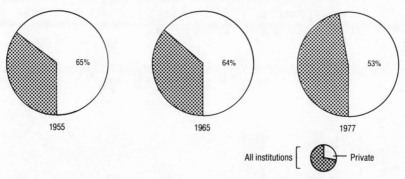

Source: Hodgkinson, 1971; National Center for Education Statistics, 1978a.

Figure 4. Enrollment in private institutions as a percentage of enrollment in all U.S. institutions of higher education, 1955, 1965, and 1977

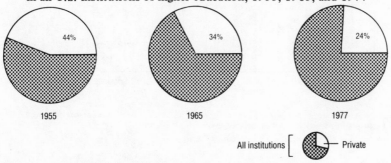

Source: American Council on Education, 1977.

2. Hodgkinson observed that, between 1947 and 1966, substantial gains were made in the number of institutions offering M.A.'s and Ph.D.'s as highest degrees and that there was a drop in the number in which the highest degree was a baccalaureate. He also noted an enormous increase in the number of institutions offering less than a B.A. as the highest degree, reflecting the great growth of two-year colleges in that period.

Since Hodgkinson's report was issued, there has been a slight decrease in the percentage of institutions offering doctorates (Figure 5). More dramatic than the increase in the proportion of institutions offering advanced degrees, however, has been the shrinkage of the proportion of institutions in which the highest degrees are four-year and master's degrees from 41.5 to 38.1 percent. The gainers appear to be nontraditional institutions and institutions offering specialized degrees.

Figure 5. Percentage distribution of U.S. institutions of higher education by level of highest degree awarded, 1970 and 1976

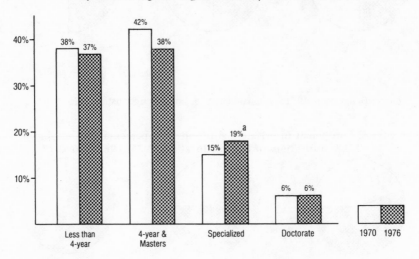

[a]Includes nontraditional institutions.
Source: Carnegie Council, 1976, Tables 1 and 2.

3. Coeducation was dominant by 1966. Between 1950 and 1966, the number of coeducational institutions increased rapidly, while the number of single-sex institutions went up slowly. During this period, there was a net increase of 424 coeducational institutions, but a net gain of only 4 men's and 16 women's institutions. Since 1966 the gain of coeducational institutions has continued. By 1978, 92.5 percent of all institutions were coeducational (Figure 6).

Figure 6. Percentage distribution of U.S. institutions of higher education by sex of student body, 1970 and 1978

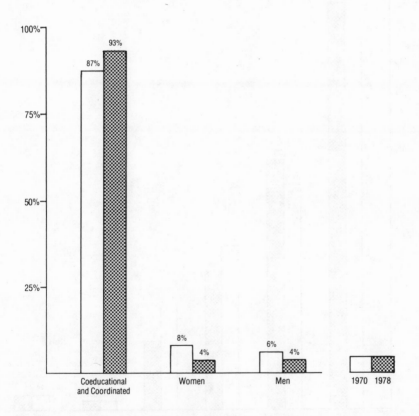

Source: National Center for Education Statistics, 1971, 1979.

4.   Another significant shift has occurred in the percentage of
     institutions with religious affiliations. I have already noted
     in this chapter that many such institutions closed between
     1970 and 1978. As may be seen in Figure 7, between
     1969-70 and 1977-78, the percentage of Protestant insti-
     tutions decreased from 19 to 16, and the percentage of
     Roman Catholic institutions was cut by nearly 36 percent.

Figure 7. Percentage distribution of U.S. institutions of higher education
by religious affiliation, 1970 and 1978

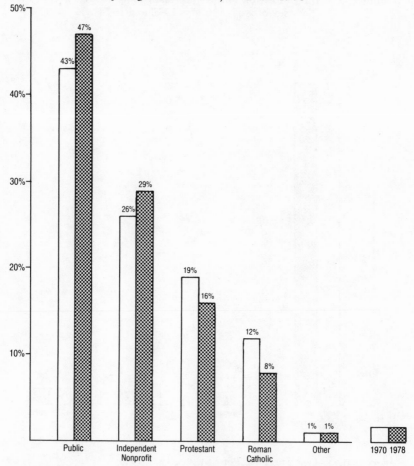

Source: National Center for Education Statistics, 1971, 1979.

Part of the explanation is the founding of increased numbers of public institutions during the period. Another reason is that many institutions with religious affiliations have changed their designation to "independent nonprofit" so that they are eligible for certain kinds of governmental and philanthropic financial assistance. However, 66 colleges with a religious affiliation, including 48 Catholic colleges, closed or merged between 1970 and 1978 (Carnegie Council, 1980, Supplement D, Table 6).

In all, 266 institutions changed classification between 1970 and 1976. These shifts can be seen in Table 27, where X's indicate the position of an institution in 1970. Some shifts result from minor changes in the definition of institutional categories that were made in 1976, but the effect of these changes was to move institutions into less rather than more comprehensive categories. Virtually all of the movement toward comprehensiveness must be recognized as occurring by virtue of changes in the character of the institutions themselves.

If changes in classification can be interpreted as signals of volatility, the greatest volatility obviously occurs among Liberal Arts Colleges and Doctorate-granting Institutions II, one-third of which changed classification between 1970 and 1976. The number of liberal arts colleges (the least comprehensive, yet most diverse, of the four-year institutions) decreased from 721 to 538, and their enrollment went from about 690,000 to 531,000. Table 27 also shows how comprehensive colleges apparently are increasing at the expense of other classes of institutions. Of the institutions represented in the table, 123 (almost half of those reclassified) were in this category in 1976. In 1970 there were 456 comprehensive colleges and universities in the United States. By 1977 there were 137 more, and they constituted 19 percent of all institutions of higher education and enrolled 30 percent of all students (Carnegie Council, 1980, p. 57).

Institutional diversity also results as new institutions are created for new constituencies. For example, in addition to the scores of already existing historically black colleges, several

Table 27. Shifts in Classification of 251 Institutions, 1970-1976

Status in 1970	Other	Two-Year Colleges	Liberal Arts Colleges II	Liberal Arts Colleges I	Comprehensive Universities & Colleges II	Comprehensive Universities & Colleges I	Doctorate-granting Universities II	Doctorate-granting Universities I	Research Universities II	Research Universities I	Total Shifts
Research Universities I									4	X	4
Research Universities II								2	X	3	5
Doctorate-granting Universities I						1	4	X	8		13
Doctorate-Granting Universities II						2	X	8			10
Comprehensive Universities & Colleges I					20	X	9	2			31
Comprehensive Universities & Colleges II	2		16		X	6		1			15
Liberal Arts Colleges I	11	1	17	X	15	5		1			40
Liberal Arts Colleges II	29	1	X	27	53	18					128
Two-Year Colleges	6	X	11		2	1					20

Source: Carnegie Commission, 1973; Carnegie Council, 1976.

new ones have opened, including Nairobi College, which opened in East Palo Alto, California, in 1969. Native American colleges established since 1960 include College of Ganado in Arizona, Flathead Valley Community College in Montana, and D.Q. University in California (which also serves Chicanos). Hispanic students are served by new institutions like César Chavez College in Oregon, Incarnate Word College and Laredo Junior College in Texas, and Hostos Community College in New York City, to name only a few.

The diversity made possible by institutions founded by older Christian denominations has recently been extended by such institutions as Oral Roberts University in Oklahoma and CBN University (Christian Broadcasting Network) in Virginia. Among the non-Christian institutions of recent foundation is Nyingma Institute for Buddhists in California.

One difficulty encountered in quantifying trends in higher education is that statistical aggregation masks a lot of variation. In the Carnegie Council's 1978 surveys of institutional adaptations to the 1970s, several questions were asked to elicit information about the extent to which certain kinds of subject matter (e.g., fine arts, humanities, business) had been added to college and university curricula. In most of the fields listed in this survey, large proportions (often 60 to 95 percent) of the officials of all types of institutions in all Carnegie classifications indicated that certain programs were in effect. These responses suggest considerable conformity in American colleges and universities. However, they do not convey the fact that an institution may offer only one course in music and none in painting, drama, the dance, or literature and still honestly say that it offers instruction in the "fine arts." Or that business education at a university is usually oriented toward management theory, but, at two-year colleges and some comprehensive colleges, business courses are concerned with accounting and secretarial skills.

The number and levels of academic degrees offered; requirements for graduation or certification; the mix of concentrations or majors, general education, and electives available; the levels of expertise found among faculty members; the availability of different learning situations and instructional technologies; and even the numbers of subjects that are taught vary widely from institution to institution.

There are also lags in institutional development. A few institutions may adopt a promising new idea as soon as it is called to their attention. But some of these same institutions may discard the innovation and begin experimenting with more promising alternatives long before other institutions begin to take the first innovation seriously. Meanwhile, there are always some institutions that simply resist change and refuse to become a part of new movements in any direction. Diversity is the inevitable consequence of this staggered experience.

Another recent development that contributes to the diversity of higher education is the addition of short-term, master's degree programs to the curricula of some liberal arts colleges. These programs not only offer differences in the levels and substance of instruction, but also scheduling alternatives, for they are often offered at night or on weekends. They also offer diversity of location, for classes may be held in downtown centers, in industrial plant facilities, or at military installations. Among institutions with such programs are Nova University in Florida, National University in California, and those in the Union of Experimenting Colleges and Universities.

Concerns and Suggestions

The diversity of American higher education is not in any immediate danger of demise, but concerns for the strength of certain kinds of institutions are justified. They include:

1. *Institutions that stand at the frontier of advanced learning and thought.* As suggested by Figure 5, doctorate-granting institutions already show signs of becoming a decreasing proportion of the nation's colleges and universities. The research functions of higher education are currently undersupported and, if undernourished in universities for too long, might be transferred to other types of institutions in our society.

2. *Institutions that give special attention to certain types of*

students. In regard to this topic, I have already noted the decreasing availability of single-sex institutions and of institutions affiliated with religious denominations. There is no virtue in segregation of any kind for its own sake, but institutions for men, women, members of minorities, and adherents to certain beliefs do offer special intellectual challenges and provide social support systems that encourage some students to achieve educational levels near the highest limits of their abilities. Higher education and the society it serves would be poorer without them.

3. *Small, experimenting, and developing institutions.* Of the 129 independent colleges and universities that closed between 1970 and 1978, 124 had less than 1,000 students (Fadil and Thrift, 1978, p. 6). This situation certainly substantiates the judgment of the Carnegie Commission (1971b, p. 6) that enrollments of 1,000 are a "peril point" and that institutions with fewer than that number can anticipate difficulties. Smallness is not in itself a virtue. Many of these institutions, however, have special and important missions. Many seminaries and conservatories are found among them. Others in the group are new and/or experimental, and some maintain high levels of quality. Such institutions would be badly missed if they were forced to close.

Some Earlier Suggestions

The Carnegie Commission and the Carnegie Council, between them, have made scores of recommendations that would maintain or increase diversity among colleges. Nine of these continue to have relevance *for the encouragement of diversity among institutions:*

1. Continue to encourage each institution to develop an explicit statement of its mission (The Carnegie Foundation for the Advancement of Teaching, *Missions of the College Curriculum,* 1977).
2. Use the power of state coordinating boards to reinforce distinctions among institutional missions (Carnegie

Commission, *The Open-Door Colleges,* 1970, *College Graduates and Jobs,* 1973a).

3. Create student assistance programs designed and administered in ways that stimulate "marketplace" responses to the diversity of student needs. Examples include portability of state grants and loans and voucher systems (Carnegie Council, *The Federal Role in Postsecondary Education,* 1975b, *The States and Private Higher Education,* 1977, and *Next Steps for the 1980s in Student Financial Aid,* 1979b).

4. Avoid rigidity in state formulas for financial support and halt the spread of increasingly detailed state controls (The Carnegie Foundation for the Advancement of Teaching, *The States and Higher Education,* 1976).

5. Support the continued existence of black colleges (Carnegie Commission, *From Isolation to Mainstream,* 1971a) and women's colleges (Carnegie Commission, *Opportunities for Women in Higher Education,* 1973d).

6. Encourage diversity within institutions by supporting innovation. For this purpose, the Carnegie Commission proposed the creation of a National Foundation for the Development of Higher Education (*Quality and Equality,* 1968). This type of activity is now carried on by the Fund for the Improvement of Postsecondary Education (FIPSE).

7. Within multicampus institutions, encourage diversity through differing emphases and programs on the various campuses (Carnegie Commission, *Priorities for Action,* 1973e).

8. Provide alternative instructional technologies so that a variety of learning experiences are available to students and so that subject matter beyond the expertise of an institution's own faculty is introduced (Carnegie Commission, *The Fourth Revolution,* 1972).

9. Develop accreditation and licensing procedures that encourage rather than discourage diversity among institutions (The Carnegie Foundation for the Advancement of Teaching, *Missions of the College Curriculum,* 1977; Carnegie Council, *Fair Practices in Higher Education,* 1979a).

For Consideration Now

To the extent that they encourage institutions to develop unique missions, induce constructive competition among institutions, free institutions from unnecessary regulation and standardization, and foster the creation of new alternatives to traditional ways of teaching and learning, all of the above recommendations continue to have merit.

Now, however, there is great need for more emphasis on the following policies:

1. Support and expansion of the research function of higher education
2. Adequate support and expansion of the Fund for the Improvement of Postsecondary Education (FIPSE), which has a good record of supporting innovation and constructive change in colleges and universities
3. Establishment of FIPSE-type agencies at the state level
4. The creation of new agencies and procedures for the support of small and developing institutions.

Considerations for the Support of Small Colleges

The fourth of the policies noted above presents difficulties. The 450 small liberal arts colleges and 230 private two-year colleges in the country are fragile and sensitive to even modest enrollment shifts and decreases in financial support. But, as I noted earlier, many of them, including some that are particularly insecure, render important services to their students and to the nation. It may be in the national interest to give special attention and help to those that are educationally sound and make a useful contribution to the diversity of American higher education. Some examples of efforts to do this follow.

Aid for developing institutions. One example of the federal government's efforts to assist small colleges is found in Section 301(a) of Title III of the Higher Education Act of 1965. Its purpose is "to strengthen the academic quality of developing institutions which have the desire and potential to make a substantial contribution to the higher education resources of our nation but which are struggling for survival

and are isolated from the main currents of academic life." The
provision was regarded by many of its original supporters as a
means by which federal support could be given to predominantly
black colleges, but the law's definition of a developing college
fits many other small colleges as well. To qualify for assistance
under the act, institutions must be legally authorized to provide
a bachelor's degree-granting program or be a community college;
be accredited or in the process of accreditation; be making
reasonable efforts to improve the quality of their teaching and
administrative staffs and their student services; and be struggling for survival for financial or other reasons.

More than $750 million has been spent on direct grants to
developing institutions since 1965. In 1977, 279 institutions
received some form of aid under the program. Of these institutions, 44 percent were black colleges; 6 percent were Hispanic
institutions; and 8 percent were Indian colleges. The remaining
42 percent of the funds went to predominantly white four-year
and two-year institutions.

Revised regulations for the Strengthening of Developing
Institutions Program were issued by the U.S. Office of Education in March 1979 (*Federal Register*, March 30, 1979,
p. 19136). Among other things, the regulations identify institutions as *developing* if: "(1) they are struggling for survival;
(2) they are isolated from the main currents of academic life;
(3) they possess the desire and potential to make a substantial
and distinctive contribution to the higher education resources
of the nation; (4) they are distinguished from other institutions
of higher education by enrolling and graduating a significant
number of economically deprived students; (5) they are making
reasonable efforts to improve the quality of their programs."

Controversy surrounds this program, because the definition
of a "developing" college is ambiguous and some critics feel
that administration of the act results in disproportionate distribution of funds to minority institutions. The U.S. General
Accounting Office called the program "unworkable" and in
need of major change (*Higher Education Daily*, Feb. 5, 1979).

In 1968, the Carnegie Commission recommended that
annual expenditures for developing institutions be increased

from $20 million to $100 million—a goal that was exceeded in 1976 when $110 million was expended. Support for gradually increasing appropriations for these institutions was also given by the Carnegie Council (1975b) in its report, *The Federal Role in Postsecondary Education.*

Per-capita formulas. When the education amendments of 1972 were being considered, attempts were made to make special treatment for small colleges a part of the package. One formula emphasized federal subsidies paid directly to institutions (rather than through student assistance). It was based on full-time equivalent enrollment calculated on credits earned and multiplied by a factor of $100 for first- and second-year students, $150 for third- and four-year students, and $200 for graduate students. The formula had special provisions for small colleges: the first 200 students would entitle an institution to an additional $300 each, and the next 100 students would entitle an institution to an additional $200 each. This proposal was not adopted. Instead, Congress provided grants, loans, and other financial assistance that made it possible for more students to attend institutions of their choice and did not put a premium on smallness for its own sake.

State assistance. Although the federal government does not assist small colleges on a per capita basis, at least two states give them special treatment. In Maryland, regional and smaller community colleges receive up to $685 more per student than do other community colleges in the state. In California, there is a differential of about $700 in state support given to smaller community colleges.

The small business model. Something like the Small Business Administration (SBA) may be needed to help small colleges in the future. The SBA, an independent federal agency, was created by the Small Business Act of 1953 to provide a formal mechanism for assisting and protecting small business interests. Essentially, it provides financial, investment, procurement, and management assistance. Its most valuable function is to provide guaranteed, direct, or immediate participation loans to help businesses finance plant construction, conversion, or expansion, or needed equipment and facilities. The SBA also provides loans for economic hardship as a result of a major disaster or as a result of a business's having had to comply with particular legal mandates. In 1977, more than $3 billion was lent to small businesses—an all-time record.

With that model in mind, consideration might be given to establishment of regional consortia of institutions, perhaps pooling some of their endowment investments in a federally protected loan fund, to assume for small colleges the role that state and local loan companies now play for small businesses. Such an agency might be called a fund for emergency and developmental support for colleges and would have responsibility for providing financial management assistance and loans for small colleges in difficulty. Direct financial assistance offered by the federal government might also be made available through these agencies on a one-time, relatively short-term basis (one to three years) for institutions with demonstrable need and promise. Such agencies could both decentralize the administration of assistance to such institutions and encourage more individualized evaluation of the needs and effectiveness of the institutions that are assisted.

A fund for emergency and developmental support might replace some of the present developing college programs financed under Title III of the Higher Education Act of 1965. It should target assistance to private institutions with fewer than 3,500 students that are demonstrably struggling for survival; need temporary assistance to overcome difficulties or to initiate programs that promise to make special contributions to the higher educational resources of the nation; and are making reasonable efforts to improve the quality of their programs.

Institutions that have as their primary mission service to members of racial minorities should by no means be excluded from the assistance of such a program, but neither should they have any priority claims on its benefits. The objective of providing direct assistance to institutions primarily because of the character of their constituencies can be more effectively served by programs specifically designed for that purpose.

No program, however, should put a premium on smallness alone. As noted earlier, institutions with less than 1,000 students are at a "peril point" (Carnegie Commission, 1971, p. 6), and, if they knowingly maintain student bodies smaller than that, they must bear an extra burden of proof that any claims they make for special assistance and support are merited. My suggestions simply acknowledge that institutions that are truly in a developmental stage or are in a position to serve special clients in special ways may need expert consultation, loans, and, in some cases, direct funding to survive. Decentralizing such assistance may not only preserve institutions that merit it, but also contribute significantly to the diversity of American higher education.

Concluding Observations

Diversity remains one of the most distinctive and valuable features of American higher education. Predictions of its imminent demise are both premature and overdrawn. Much of the diversity among institutions that has been lost in recent years has been offset by increasing diversity of programs within institutions as they become larger and more comprehensive.

This is not to say, however, that diversity is fully secure. It cannot help but be reduced under the force of any trend that centralizes decision making in higher education. It also cannot help but be reduced by any significant contraction of an important sector in higher education.

Fears for the diversity represented by research universities are real, mainly because research, their most distinctive activity, recently has been endangered by neglect and, perhaps, overdependence on a single source of funding. The basic strategy required for protecting the diversity these institutions provide is the maintenance of adequate and reliable levels of federal government support for research.

Fears for the diversity represented by institutions that serve special student bodies are also real. Ironically, they have been made real, at least in part, by the egalitarian sentiments of the 1960s that frowned on separatism of any sort. Fortunately, some strong educational statesmen continue to defend the roles of special-constituent institutions and resist their dissolution. They may carry a heavy burden, however, as the choice between survival and giving up special missions becomes tougher.

Since most of these institutions are in the private sector, the generosity of former students, religious sponsors, and private philanthropy may be vital to the outcome.

Fears of the diversity of education offered by small colleges are the most real of all. Most of the *institutional* diversity, as opposed to *internal* diversity, that exists in the country is to be found in these institutions. Many of them are adventurous and experimental and are learning lessons through their experience that benefit all of higher education. It is for them, perhaps, that special mechanisms and assitance may be most urgently needed if diversity is to be protected in the years ahead.

6

Adaptations to Decreasing Enrollments

In many ways, the 1970s were good years for American higher education. The confrontations that punctuated student unrest in the 1960s became less frequent and less disruptive. Students became more serious about their studies than they had been for some time. Public support persisted. The level of annual income for higher education was not only sustained but increased by 85 percent—from $21.5 billion in 1970 to $39.7 billion in 1976 (U.S. Bureau of the Census, 1978, p. 166). Enrollment increased from 8.6 million students to 11 million students in the same six years (ibid., p. 162). Why, then, is this decade characterized so frequently and by so many as one of reduced expectations for higher education?

Part of the answer can be found in the scars left by student unrest. During the campus turbulence, colleges were challenged by student rebels, by some of their own faculty members, and by many state and national politicians to define what they were trying to do, who they were trying to serve, and what contributions they intended to make to equality among people and to peace, security, and freedom in a troubled world. Such questions had been asked before but were tougher in the 1960s because many assumptions about campus consensus had been shattered. The case for the colleges was also challenged by the well-publicized specter of an emerging social class made up of the educated unemployed. As overdrawn as that vision was, it haunted the campuses and seemed to weaken one of the strongest arguments colleges had going for them—that they provided the best way for men and women to enter productive and rewarding careers.

In addition, inflation drove higher education costs per student up from $2,450 a year in 1970 to $3,530 a year in 1976 (U.S. Bureau of the Census, 1978, pp. 162 and 166)—an increase of 44 percent—and put the leaders of higher education on the defensive. The rising costs had to be met, whatever the resistence might be from students and their parents, by increasing tuition and student fees and imposing higher taxes to finance larger government appropriations for education. Colleges and university officials were encouraged by politicians, by parents of students, and by many others to believe that the outer limit of public tolerance for increased costs lay immediately beyond the next tuition hike or the next budget increase. Restraint in planning and in formulating demands was the prudent, inevitable (if unappealing) response.

Long-range enrollment forecasts also restrained expansionist impulses. There is no avoiding the demographic certainty that the number of 18- to 24-year-olds in the nation's population will decrease by 23 percent by 1997 and that enrollments in the nation's colleges will decrease as a result (Carnegie Council, 1980). It is not yet certain how sharp these decreases will be, because there may be offsetting factors, such as increasing enrollments of older students, part-time students, and students from certain ethnic minority groups.[1] But some institutions are already experiencing decreases, and the mere anticipation of enrollment decline in the future has been affecting policy making in higher education for several years.

Policies To Increase Enrollments

Thus far, many more colleges and universities have lived with enrollment growth than have experienced decline. Enrollment has held steady, increased, or fluctuated but "mostly increased" at more than three-fourths of American institutions of higher education in the past few years (Table 28).

---

[1]The Carnegie Council (1980) expects a decrease of between 5 and 15 percent by the year 2000.

Table 28. Trends in full-time equivalent (FTE) enrollment in colleges and universities in 1969-70 to 1977-78 by Carnegie classification, in percentages

	All institutions	Research Universities		Doctorate-granting Institutions		Comprehensive Colleges and Universities		Liberal Arts Colleges		Two-Year Colleges
		I	II	I	II	I	II	I	II	
All institutions										
Steady increase	41%	33%	49%	39%	42%	37%	40%	16%	36%	47%
Up and down, mostly up	22	8	9	21	7	25	15	21	23	22
Little or no change	16	42	25	25	19	17	18	42	16	10
Up and down, mostly down	15	6	5	5	25	14	15	21	18	15
Steady decrease	7	5	8	10	0	6	11.	0	7	7
Other	0	6	3	0	7	0	0	0	0	0
Public institutions										
Steady increase	49	36	58	42	35	37	33		38	55
Up and down, mostly up	20	16	4	23	12	26	20		50	19
Little or no change	11	36	19	23	24	16	13		13	14
Up and down, mostly down	14	4	8	8	24	14	20		13	13
Steady decrease	6	4	12	4	0	7	15		0	5
Other	5	0	0	11	0	0	0		0	0
Private institutions										
Steady increase	30	30	31	31	57	38	47	16	36	36
Up and down, mostly up	23	0	15	0	26	11	21	23	35	23
Little or no change	23	50	46	31	14	18	23	42	24	23
Up and down, mostly down	17	5	0	0	29	14	11	21	18	19
Steady decrease	8	5	0	23	0	5	8	0	7	15
Other	0	10	0	0	2	0	0	0	0	0

Note: Percentages may not add to 100 because of rounding.
Source: Carnegie Council Surveys, 1978.

The growth in the size of the college-age population of the country is primarily responsible for increased enrollments. But other factors, including certain institutional policy decisions designed to attract and hold students, are also involved. Thus, when they are asked to explain enrollment growth at their own institutions, college and university officials frequently mention the development of new facilities; changes in the curriculum that appeal to new groups of students; conscious efforts to recruit older students and students from minority groups; and the introduction of continuing education programs. Newer colleges report that enrollment growth occurred just because they became better established and attracted more students as they became better known. Colleges that moved to new locations often showed similar growth. And improved transportation or the building of freeways made many campuses more accessible to students living in the areas they serve.

Five of these policies deserve further discussion, because each of them is an important factor in enrollment growth at more than 50 percent of the nation's campuses (Table 29).

Table 29. Percentage of all institutions reporting some
or substantial increase in enrollment caused by
selected policy changes from 1969-70 to 1977-78

More aggressive or expanded recruiting	62%
Increased financial aid to students	61
Expanded high-demand programs (new majors, work education, and so on)	59
More publicity, community awareness	58
Expanded evening or weekend programs	50

Source: Carnegie Council Surveys, 1978.

Changes in Admissions and Recruiting

The most direct method of increasing enrollments is to persuade more people to enroll as students, and this course has been adopted by 62 percent of the country's institutions of higher education. To direct this effort, 60 percent of all institutions increased the number of staff members engaged in admissions and recruitment activities by 10 percent between 1969-70 and 1977-78, and 36 percent expect to do the same between

1977-78 and 1985-86. Liberal Arts Colleges II are particularly likely to place more emphasis on student recruitment, but the Comprehensive Universities and Colleges II and Doctorate-granting Universities II also have beefed up recruiting efforts substantially (Carnegie Council Surveys, 1978).

One consequence of these recent trends is that prospective students are finding it easier to find a place in college. One-half of all institutions now accept between 90 and 100 percent of freshman applicants (Carnegie Council Surveys, 1978). The traditionally "open-door" community colleges make up a large proportion (68 percent) of these institutions, but they are now encountering some competition from Liberal Arts Colleges II, 41 percent of which also admit more than 90 percent of their freshman applicants. The modal acceptance rate for other colleges and universities is between 70 and 80 percent of their applicants, and the percentage of applicants admitted has increased even at the highly selective Liberal Arts Colleges I.

More than 70 percent of all private institutions, for example, accept and enroll able students in college prior to high school graduation. Similar percentages of comprehensive universities and colleges and selective liberal arts colleges now have early notification systems for the students they decide to admit. At many of these institutions, students are also guaranteed admission as soon as they are selected, even though they may choose to delay matriculation (Table 30).

Many colleges and universities also give entering students advanced standing on the bases of successfully completed College Level Educational Placement (CLEP) examinations or other placement tests; courses successfully completed at other colleges or universities; courses successfully completed at vocational-technical or business schools; or through assessment of prior experiential learning acquired outside a school or college (Table 30).

This review of changes in admissions procedures in the 1970s indicates that colleges have responded to two trends. The first trend is toward greater flexibility and innovation in all programs and procedures in higher education. Some of the changes made for this purpose fall into a category popularly

Table 30. Percentage of institutions of higher education with selected policies for admission of students and awarding of academic credit, by Carnegie classification, in 1969-70 and 1977-78

	Research Universities I		Research Universities II		Doctorate-granting Universities I		Doctorate-granting Universities I	
	1969-70	1977-78	1969-70	1977-78	1969-70	1977-78	1969-70	1977-78
Campus awards credit or grants advanced standing on basis of:								
Courses successfully completed at other colleges or universities	97%	100%	94%	100%	100%	100%	96%	100%
CLEP examinations	45	71	29	75	37	82	22	97
Advanced placement tests	97	100	86	92	90	95	58	97
Examinations created at campus	69	79	71	83	61	75	58	83
Courses successfully completed at vocational-technical or business schools	11	16	20	35	15	28	16	37
Assessment of prior experiental learning acquired outside a school or college	8	11	6	38	5	26	13	49
Campus admissions policy includes:								
Early decision (selected students notified of acceptance well in advance of other applicants)	42	58	32	40	41	48	62	72
Early admission (students accepted and enrolled in college prior to high school graduation)	63	79	60	72	53	75	69	89
Deferred admission (students guaranteed admission but permitted to delay matriculation)	50	55	52	61	41	58	42	51

Table 30 (Continued). Percentages of institutions of higher education with selected policies for admission of students and awarding of academic credit in 1969-70 and 1977-78

	Comprehensive Universities & Colleges I		Comprehensive Universities & Colleges II		Liberal Arts Colleges I		Liberal Arts Colleges II	
	1969-70	1977-78	1969-70	1977-78	1969-70	1977-78	1969-70	1977-78
Campus awards credit or grants advanced standing on basis of:								
Courses successfully completed at other colleges or universities	95%	99%	95%	98%	94%	96%	97%	100%
CLEP examinations	39	93	33	89	28	66	33	94
Advanced placement tests	73	88	69	85	78	87	70	89
Examinations created at campus	55	79	58	73	65	75	54	72
Courses successfully completed at vocational-technical or business schools	42	54	30	45	11	19	34	55
Assessment of prior experiental learning acquired outside a school or college	14	45	10	42	6	19	9	43
Campus admissions policy includes:								
Early decision (selected students notified of acceptance well in advance of other applicants)	44	48	47	57	74	87	43	51
Early admission (students accepted and enrolled in college prior to high school graduation)	49	73	48	70	63	87	48	77
Deferred admission (students guaranteed admission put permitted to delay matriculation)	40	60	46	59	57	83	41	49

Table 30 (Continued). Percentages of institutions of higher education with selected policies for admission of students and awarding of academic credit in 1969-70 and 1977-78

	Two-year Colleges		All institutions	
	1969-70	1977-78	1969-70	1977-78
Campus awards credit or grants advanced standing on basis of:				
Courses successfully completed at other colleges or universities	95%	98%	96%	98%
CLEP examinations	35	78	35	84
Advanced placement tests	38	71	58	81
Examinations created at campus	48	83	53	79
Courses successfully completed at vocational-technical or business schools	50	68	39	56
Assessment of prior experiential learning acquired outside a school or college	19	43	14	41
Campus admissions policy includes:				
Early decision (selected students notified of acceptance well in advance of other applicants)	30	39	40	47
Early admission (students accepted and enrolled in college prior to high school graduation)	43	69	48	73
Deferred admission (students guaranteed admission but permitted to delay matriculation)	37	40	41	50

Source: Carnegie Council Surveys, 1978.

called "nontraditional" in the 1970s. Not all of them have caught on. For example, the use of advanced placement tests, admission on the basis of CLEP scores, and admission and placement based on an assessment of experiential learning acquired outside a school or colleges are practices found at a surprisingly large number of institutions, but in many instances —particularly at small colleges—they affect only three or four students a year.

The second trend involves the admission of new types of students. The time when recruiting emphasis was almost entirely on high school graduates between the ages of 18 and 22 is long gone. Attention is now given to enrolling students even before they leave high school, to ethnic minority students, to low-income students, to students over 22 years old, to students for off-campus programs, to evening students, and to previous college dropouts. Some colleges have been showing an increased interest in such students since 1969-70; others will seek such students out for the first time in the 1980s.

Table 31 presents information about the recruiting emphases of American colleges and universities since 1969-70 and the expected emphases in the coming five or six years. One change it makes particularly clear is a shift in recruiting efforts from those directed to members of minority groups to those directed to adult and part-time students. The 1960s and most of the 1970s were years of "affirmative action" on the American campuses, and strong efforts were made to open college doors to members of minority groups. The passage of the education amendments of 1972 made more financial assistance available for these students, and the continuing development of community colleges provided more places for them to study. By the end of the 1970s, the participation of white women and of blacks of both sexes in higher education had increased to the point where the rate of their attendance approached that of white males. The Carnegie Council (1980) now expects the participation of both of these groups to match or exceed that of majority males in the coming decades. Extraordinary efforts may still be needed to insure the adequate participation of Hispanics and low-income blacks, but many

Table 31. Percentage of institutions of higher education indicating more emphasis on recruiting selected groups of prospective students, by Carnegie classification, since 1969-70 and anticipated in 1985-86 compared to 1977-78

	Research Universities I		Research Universities II		Doctorate-granting Universities I		Doctorate-granting Universities II	
	1970-1978	1978-1986	1970-1978	1978-1986	1970-1978	1978-1986	1970-1978	1978-1986
Evening students	37	39	42	67	56	62	63	61
Ethnic minority students	89	62	84	67	82	54	89	59
Adults over 22	40	58	76	79	70	69	79	86
Students for off-campus programs	48	38	47	71	82	92	62	56
Low-income students	46	32	42	45	50	40	35	37
Transfer students	49	54	55	65	67	54	65	71
Students enrolled before graduation from high school	22	24	24	22	33	30	33	18
Traditional students (high school graduates, 18-22 years old)	34	31	26	40	21	16	35	43
Previous dropouts	16	27	16	45	15	23	0	29

Table 31 (Continued). Percentage of institutions of higher education indicating more emphasis on recruiting selected groups of prospective students, by Carnegie classification, since 1969-70 and anticipated in 1985-86 compared to 1977-78

	Comprehensive Universities & Colleges I		Comprehensive Universities & Colleges II		Liberal Arts Colleges I		Liberal Arts Colleges II	
	1970-1978	1978-1986	1970-1978	1978-1986	1970-1978	1978-1986	1970-1978	1978-1986
Evening students	67	77	63	73	77	69	67	79
Ethnic minority students	71	54	67	61	59	49	63	60
Adults over 22	50	82	62	48	55	58	77	78
Students for off-campus programs	73	95	66	62	36	31	53	66
Low-income students	40	25	45	37	33	16	35	35
Transfer students	63	60	71	66	64	60	65	78
Students enrolled before graduation from high school	34	31	26	40	21	16	35	43
Traditional students (high school graduates, 18-22 years old)	45	45	38	33	41	46	31	25
Previous dropouts	26	38	32	39	1	16	24	37

Table 31 (Continued). Percentage of institutions of higher education indicating more emphasis on recruiting selected groups of prospective students, by Carnegie classification, since 1969-70 and anticipated in 1985-86 compared to 1977-78

	Two-Year Colleges		All institutions	
	1970-1978	1978-1986	1970-1978	1978-1986
Evening students	72	72	67	73
Ethnic minority students	60	57	65	57
Adults over 22	84	78	64	78
Students for off-campus programs	63	74	63	65
Low-income students	57	48	47	39
Transfer students	19	27	46	49
Students enrolled before graduation from high school	41	43	35	38
Traditional students (high school graduates, 18-22 years old)	28	41	34	38
Previous dropouts	39	50	31	43

Source: Carnegie Council Surveys, 1978.

of the barriers to members of these groups have already come down. The percentage of colleges and universities with special admissions policies for disadvantaged, minority, or low-income students has increased substantially since 1969-70. Only in two-year colleges and in private Research Universities II has there been a decline in the use of such policies (Carnegie Council Surveys, 1978). Recruiting no longer requires precedent-breaking measures. The enrollment of qualified members of minority groups is sufficiently important to the health of student-hungry colleges and universities that it is unlikely that they will be ignored in the years ahead. Fewer colleges and universities now anticipate placing as great an emphasis on members of minorities in their recruiting efforts as was the case between 1969-70 and 1978, but this does not mean that policies and practices that are now in place to encourage attendance by such students will be abandoned.

This is a good place to observe that not all of the efforts to seek out new students are inspired by a drive to build enrollments. Not enough credit is given to colleges and universities whose concern for the "new" students primarily reflects their commitment to provide educational opportunities to members of ethnic and socioeconomic groups who have previously been denied them or who now have special needs for higher education. But the fact remains that recruiting students from expanded pools of prospects is a matter not only of social conscience but also of minimizing the losses that seem inevitable because too few babies were born in the 1960s to produce for the 1980s the numbers of prospective traditional students to which college recruiters have become accustommed.

Apparently out of resignation to these demographic realities, college and university officials expect the enrollment of traditional students—those 18 to 22 years old who are high school graduates—to take care of itself. Only among doctorate-granting universities do we find a majority of institutions that indicate they plan to give increased emphasis to recruiting such students; these institutions may seek traditional students to offset anticipated losses in graduation enrollments. More than 60 percent of both the Liberal Arts Colleges II and the two-year colleges report that they intend to give *less* emphasis to such students in their recruiting efforts. These open-access institutions may well believe that they have already exhausted the pool of traditional students that they have usually served.

In all institutions except Research Universities I and Comprehensive Universities and Colleges I, efforts to recruit adults over 22 years old have increased. Interest in these students is particularly strong in two-year colleges and Liberal Arts Colleges II, Doctorate-granting Universities II, and Research Universities II, and still greater emphasis will be placed on adult student recruiting by these institutions in the future. Even the Comprehensive Universities and Colleges I, which have been somewhat less likely than other institutions to seek adult students in the past, now plan to increase emphasis on recruiting them in the future; officials of 82 percent of these institutions report such expectations.

Reaching out for new clienteles has been accompanied by a greater openness and aggressiveness in college and university recruiting. Advertising in newspapers, magazines, and other mass media is more common than it was ten years ago and is used by more than three-quarters of all two-year and liberal arts colleges to attract students. It is also used by 73 percent of the private Comprehensive Universities and Colleges I. Universities of all kinds are less likely than other institutions to advertise for students. Even so, 47 percent of the private Doctorate-granting Universities I and 57 percent of private Doctorate-granting Universities II use advertising. Moreover, 60 percent or more of the private research universities and Doctorate-granting Universities I also use the College Entrance Examination Board's student search service to find qualified students (Carnegie Council Surveys, 1978).

Increased Student Financial Aid

Officials of American colleges and universities rank the availability of financial aid to students second, after increased student recruiting activity, as the most frequent cause of enrollment increase in institutions of higher education (Table 29).

Between 1969 and 1978, federal expenditures for student aid programs increased from $1 billion to $3.2 billion in constant dollars (Carnegie Council, 1979b, p. 69). In the same period, the dollar awards of state-funded, need-based scholarships and grants increased from $221 million to $449 million in constant dollars (ibid., p. 73). The student aid that institutions provide from private sources increased from $635 million to $753 million in constant dollars between 1969 and 1976 (ibid., p. 74).

Student aid is important enough to the overwhelming majority of colleges and universities that they set aside some of their unrestricted revenues to provide scholarships or fee waivers to their needier students. Private institutions are particularly likely to pursue this policy. Of the private institutions that had steadily increasing enrollments since 1969-70, all of the research and doctorate-granting universities, 84 percent of the comprehensive universities and colleges, 75 percent of the liberal arts colleges, and 69 percent of the two-year colleges report such allocations in 1978 (Carnegie Council Surveys, 1978). At public institutions with increasing enrollments since 1969-70, only about one-third (37 percent) of the two-year colleges and no liberal arts colleges follow this practice. But it is reported by officials in 75 percent of the comprehensive colleges and universities and 79 percent of the public universities with increasing enrollments.

In Table 32, which presents information on the share of tuition and fee income allocated for student grants and tuition waivers, one can see that the percentage of all institutions reporting shares of between 0 and 9 percent has been declining over the past 10 years, and the percentage of institutions reporting shares of between 10 and 34 percent has been increasing. Apparently some institutions decreased the shares of tuition and fee income allocated for student aid between 1968 and 1973 but began to increase the shares again in the past five years. But the data in the three parts of Table 32 are supplied by unequal numbers of institutions, and there is a strong possibility that the total level of student assistance

Table 32. Allocation of shares of tuition and fee income for student grants and tuition waivers in 1978 at institutions of higher education, in percentage of responding institutions, by Carnegie classification

	Research Universities		Doctorate-granting Institutions		Comprehensive Colleges and Universities		Liberal Arts Colleges		Two-Year Colleges	All institutions
	I	II	I	II	I	II	I	II		
Percentage of current budget										
0-9%	30%	62%	67%	52%	57%	61%	25%	50%	62%	52%
10-24%	60	26	26	48	43	39	75	39	19	41
25-34%	5	6	7	0	0	0	0	6	12	4
Over 34%	5	6	0	0	0	0	0	6	7	3
Percentage of budget 5 years ago										
0-9%	19	73	68	72	76	70	37	61	74	64
10-24%	63	19	33	29	25	30	63	23	16	30
25-34%	6	0	0	0	0	0	0	16	0	2
Over 34%	13	8	0	0	0	0	0	0	9	4
Percentage of budget 10 years ago										
0-9%	37	60	45	48	60	68	25	82	74	65
10-24%	54	30	29	29	39	32	76	18	16	32
25-34%	0	10	26	24	0	0	0	0	0	0
Over 34%	9	0	0	0	0	0	0	0	9	3

Note: Officials of colleges and universities were asked to supply this information if it was readily available. Information for the current budget was supplied by 582 institutions; for budgets 5 years ago by 426 institutions; for budgets 10 years ago by 374 institutions.
Source: Carnegie Council Surveys, 1978.

from tuition income has actually increased significantly. The trend therefore deserves further study. If the level actually is increasing, it offsets the effect of increases in tuitions made by most institutions to meet the rising costs of general operation.

Publicity and Community Awareness

Public relations were once aimed principally at fund-raising targets and at improving an institution's general good will. It is now the fourth most frequently reported reason for increased enrollments (Table 29), having contributed to attracting more students to 83 percent of the country's colleges and universities. As an example of the importance of public relations in enrollment, I cite the hopes that the president of a small college in Oklahoma attached to the possibility that a shoe manufacturer in New York might use his campus as a setting for some national TV commercials. At the same institution, a handsome new art museum recently opened. Quite aside from the appropriateness of this facility on a liberal arts college campus (and particularly on a campus that was once home for one of the nation's most distinguished painters and art collectors), the new museum is also regarded as an attraction that will bring the general public onto the campus. Both of these forms of exposure could be very important to an isolated Roman Catholic two-year college that is stubbornly resisting pressures to abandon its traditional dedication to the liberal arts, yet still needs 100 to 150 more students in order to be secure and optimally effective.

Here is another example of the value of public attention. When the Carnegie Commission on Higher Education published a profile of "invisible colleges" (Astin and Lee, 1972)—small institutions with less selective admissions policies—it struck a sensitive nerve. Although nothing was implied by the term "invisible" other than that most of these institutions are not well known, protests and disclaimers were immediately filed by many small colleges throughout the country. For them, visibility was linked to the notion of prestige and calling attention to its absence was regarded as a slander. It is doubtful that the protests would have been so vehement if public attention were not regarded by colleges and universities as instrumental in sustaining enrollment growth and financial contributions.

Expanding High-Demand Programs—Increasing the Options

One way for colleges and universities to attract and keep students is to develop the curricula and instructional modes that have the strongest student appeal. In our survey of institutional adaptations to the 1970s, 68 percent of the officials of colleges and universities indicate that expanded high-demand program options—including new majors, work education and the like—caused some increase or substantial increase in their enrollments.

In defiance of the unfounded and utterly false idea that a college curriculum is impossible to change, at most institutions it is changing all of the time in response to new student interests and the changing expertise of faculty members. Such changes inevitably alter the options available for students.

Table 33 provides a general overview of the American college curriculum in 1978. Looking at it, one is at once struck by what appears to be homogeneity of the course and program offerings of the different types of institutions. But the areas of instruction are broadly defined, and an enormous range of variation is possible within each subject. For example, several of the subjects under "professional studies creditable toward a baccalaureate or higher degree" differ considerably in the levels of professionalism achieved by the students that pursue them. As mentioned earlier, in universities, "business" may stress the theory and practice of management; in other colleges, it may be more occupationally oriented—secretarial skills and accounting. "Health Sciences" may also include areas of study for future technicians and health care assistants rather than for prospective nurses, pharmacists, or medical doctors.

The principal value of Table 33 is not that it shows all of the differences among subjects as taught at different types of institutions but that it shows the general differentiation of function among institutional types. Arts and sciences are taught at all institutions of higher education; they are encountered somewhat less frequently in two-year colleges than in the four-year institutions because many two-year colleges are devoted to specialized technical programs. The research and doctorate-granting institutions predominate among those that offer professional studies creditable toward a baccalaureate or higher degree; and the two-year colleges predominate in programs of occupational studies leading to certificates or degrees below the baccalaureate.

To examine the relationship between enrollment and the curriculum, the staff of the Carnegie Council determined whether, between 1970 and 1978, enrollments increased or decreased in the subject areas listed in Table 33 and whether, between 1978 and 1986, college officials expect them to increase or decrease (Table 34). These results can be compared with the recent college and university experiences and future plans to add or drop courses and programs in the various fields of study shown in Table 35.

In many fields of study, enrollment increases and decreases tend to cancel each other out in the sense that approximately the same percentages of institutions experience change in each direction (Table 34). In arts and sciences, that seems to be the case in mathematics and the physical sciences. It does not happen, however, in any of the professional fields in which instruction leads to a baccalaureate degree or beyond, or in prebaccalaureate professional and occupational programs.

Even in the fields where the percentages of institutions reporting increases and decreases are about the same, however, there are institutional variations worth noting. For example, it is primarily in the private institutions, particularly in universities (except for Research Universities I and Doctorate-granting Universities II), in Liberal Arts Colleges II, and in Two-Year Colleges that the percentage of institutions reporting *increased* enrollment in the fine arts exceeds the percentage reporting decreased enrollment between 1970 and 1978. The reason for this difference is not immediately obvious. I suspect one reason is that the fine arts are regarded as "frills" by public policy makers and historically have been concentrated in private academies and conservatories. They are also regarded, however, as "popular" studies and therefore may be introduced on campuses simply to attract students. But interest in the arts is not

Table 33. Percentage of institutions offering courses in selected subject areas, by Carnegie classification, 1978

	All institutions (number)	All institutions	Research Universities I	Research Universities II	Doctorate-granting Universities I	Doctorate-granting Universities II	Comprehensive Universities & Colleges I	Comprehensive Universities & Colleges II	Liberal Arts Colleges I	Liberal Arts Colleges II	Two-Year Colleges
Arts and sciences (all degree levels)											
Fine arts	2,205	89%	97%	97%	96%	97%	96%	95%	96%	98%	80%
Humanities	2,279	92	100	97	100	100	98	98	100	100	84
Foreign languages	2,035	82	100	97	96	100	98	95	98	90	68
Social sciences	2,342	95	100	100	100	100	100	100	100	100	88
Biological sciences	2,299	93	100	100	100	100	100	100	100	94	87
Physical sciences	2,285	92	100	97	100	100	100	98	100	90	88
Mathematics	2,316	94	100	100	100	100	100	100	100	94	88
Other arts and sciences	1,564	63	87	78	84	83	81	69	47	55	58
Professional studies creditable toward a baccalaureate or higher degree											
Engineering	909	37	90	80	60	47	38	23	15	14	45
Education	1,734	70	90	77	89	100	96	95	72	96	44
Business	1,897	77	90	94	95	97	95	92	49	87	64
Legal, judicial, police	1,032	42	84	61	63	63	51	38	13	28	44
Health sciences (medicine, nursing, and so on)	1,466	59	92	78	73	79	74	59	34	59	54
All other (architecture, agriculture, and so on)	811	33	76	75	56	60	38	17	4	18	38

Occupational studies leading to certificate or degree below the baccalaureate										
Engineering and natural science technologies	969	39	13	17	22	33	26	17	0	12	66
Business and commerce	1,450	59	11	14	33	53	43	40	4	37	87
Public service-related	1,060	43	5	11	33	32	28	27	2	26	66
Health services	1,189	48	21	31	33	47	43	24	9	25	70
All other (data processing, and so on)	1,326	54	16	28	35	44	53	37	28	24	76

Source: Carnegie Council Surveys, 1978.

Table 34. Percentage of institutions reporting changes in total enrollment in selected subject areas, 1969-70 to 1977-78 and anticipated from 1977-78 to 1985-86

	Changes in percentage of total enrollment from 1969-70 to 1972-78			Changes expected in percentage of total enrollment from 1977-78 to 1978-86		
	Increase	Little or no change	Decrease	Increase	Little or no change	Decrease
Arts and sciences (all degree levels)						
Fine arts	38%	36%	26%	27%	60%	13%
Humanities	19	36	46	19	63	17
Foreign languages	7	25	68	13	62	25
Social sciences	37	39	24	34	56	10
Biological sciences	47	39	14	36	57	6
Physical sciences	27	47	26	26	66	9
Mathematics	28	45	26	30	62	8
Other arts and sciences	23	59	18	18	73	9
Professional studies creditable toward a baccalaureate or higher degree						
Engineering	39	50	11	34	62	3
Education	19	37	44	13	63	24
Business	84	13	3	64	34	2
Legal, justice, police	65	32	3	36	60	4
Health sciences (medicine, nursing, and so on)	77	21	2	53	45	2
All other (architecture, agriculture, and so on)	38	60	3	22	75	2

Occupational studies leading to certificate or degree below the baccalaureate

Engineering and natural science technologies	51	39	10	42	56	3
Business and commerce	65	29	6	54	44	2
Public service-related	59	37	4	51	45	3
Health service	71	28	1	49	48	3
All other (data processing, and so on)	63	36	1	56	43	1

Note: Percentages are based on the number of institutions that offer courses and programs in each subject area (see Table 32). Percentages may not add to 100 because of rounding.

Source: Carnegie Council Surveys, 1978.

Table 35. Percentage of institutions dropping, adding, expecting to drop, or expecting to add courses or programs in selected subject areas, 1970 to 1978 and 1977-78 to 1985-86

	Dropped between 1970 and 1978	Expect to drop 1978 to 1986	Added between 1970 and 1978	Expect to add 1978 to 1986
Arts and sciences				
Fine arts	8%	3%	37%	20%
Humanities	14	1	24	14
Foreign languages	66	12	12	8
Social sciences	6	2	35	20
Biological sciences	7	1	31	18
Physical sciences	16	2	21	12
Mathematics	5	1	26	13
Other arts and sciences	6	*	23	13
Professional studies creditable toward a baccalaureate or higher degree				
Engineering	4	1	43	24
Education	13	5	37	20
Business	4	*	55	38
Legal, judicial, police	2	*	67	36
Health sciences (medicine, nursing, and so on)	3	0	65	43
All other (architecture, and so on)	2	0	37	22
Occupational studies leading to certificate or degree below the baccalaureate				
Engineering and natural science technologies	3	3	49	35
Business and commerce	4	2	56	41
Public service-related	6	1	66	52
Health services	2	1	71	64
All other (data processing, and so on)	2	0	54	42

*Less than .05 percent.
Note: Percentages for column 1 are based on the number of institutions that said they dropped courses or programs between 1970 and 1978. Percentages for columns 2, 3, and 4 are based on the number of institutions that reported they offered courses and programs in each subject area in 1978 (see Table 33).
Source: Carnegie Council Surveys, 1978.

exclusively found in private institutions—83 percent of all of the officials responding to the Carnegie Council's 1978 survey rank the fine arts as of "great or moderate" importance.

The social sciences are another subject area in which high proportions ot enrollments are reported. They appear to be particularly strong in private institutions in which the highest degree awarded is below the doctorate level. The reason for this increase probably has something to do with the increasing role of government and social institutions in the lives of people in modern industrial societies and the possibility that the social sciences now offer an alternative to the law as preparation for public service and management careers. Whatever the reasons may be, 40 percent of all institutions added social sciences programs between 1970 and 1978, and 28 percent plan to add them before 1986.

The humanities and foreign languages, as everyone is well aware by now, were big losers of enrollments between 1970 and 1978. As many as 100 percent of the private doctorate-granting universities and 94 percent of the public institutions in that category report enrollment decreases in languages. Moreover, two-thirds of all institutions report that they dropped foreign language courses between 1970 and 1978, and 12 percent say that they expect to drop foreign language programs between 1978 and 1986 (Table 35). But there is a spiral situation here. The more programs that are dropped, the more enrollments will decrease in the fields where the drops occur, and the more that enrollments decrease, the more programs will be dropped. The cause of enrollment decline by field, therefore, is only partially found in the choices of students. Some of it lies in the decisions of colleges and universities in the 1960s to relax or remove certain courses, including languages, from the list of those that students had to take in order to receive degrees or advanced standing.

The humanities may be a case in point. Large percentages of institutions (up to 78 in the case of public Research Universities I and 83 in private Doctorate-granting Institutions II) report enrollment decreases in these subjects. But colleges and universities have heavy commitments to tenured faculty in the

humanities and appear to be determined to preserve them as
a part of their curricula in spite of consumer pressures to
abandon them. Between 1970 and 1978, only 14 percent of all
institutions had eliminated courses or had dropped programs
in the humanities. Only 1 percent of the institutions that had
humanities courses or programs in 1978 say they intend to
drop programs in that field by 1986. Both percentages are far
outweighed, however, by the 24 percent of the institutions
that added humanities programs between 1970 and 1978 and
the 14 percent that expect to add humanities programs between 1978 and 1986 (Table 35).

In the case of professional studies creditable toward a
baccalaureate or higher degree, the most dramatic change has
been the sharp decline in enrollments in education. Enrollment
decreases in education occurred in all types of institutions except public Two-Year Colleges, and increases are reported only
in private Comprehensive Universities and Colleges II. Thirteen
percent of all colleges dropped programs in education between
1970 and 1978, and 20 percent expect to drop education programs between 1978 and 1986. In view of this record of decreasing enrollments, it may seem surprising that 31 percent of
the colleges and universities added education programs in the
1970s, and 21 percent expect to add them in the next few
years. These expectations may reflect hopes for an improving
market for teachers in the coming decades as fewer college
graduates compete for the available teaching jobs and the birthrate that declined so sharply during the Vietnam war years
begins to increase and more children begin to enter school.

The concentration of programs that provide instruction in
occupational studies leading to certificates or degrees below the
baccalaureate is found in two-year and public liberal arts colleges and in some of the doctorate-granting and comprehensive
institutions. But vocational preparation is now accepted as an
important mission by almost 9 out of 10 colleges and universities of all types. Even at the most "academic" institutions,
Research Universities I and Liberal Arts Colleges I, more than
60 percent of the officials responding to the Carnegie Council
1978 survey rank vocational preparation as of "great or moderate"

importance to their institutions. But that judgment is much more typically rendered by two-year colleges (96 percent) and comprehensive colleges and universities (89 percent).

Four special components of the curriculum were much discussed in the 1970s. They were courses of instruction about ethnic minority interests or roles, breadth requirements, interdisciplinary studies, and compensatory or remedial education in such basic learning skills as reading, writing, and arithmetic. One of the things the Carnegie Council hoped to learn in its 1978 surveys was something about the status of such programs as the 1970s came to a close. The sources of our information were the college and university presidents:

- Forty-eight percent of them report that ethnic studies had become more important than they were in 1969-70, and 59 percent rank them as of "great or moderate" importance in 1978
- General education ("breadth") requirements are ranked as being of "great or moderate" importance by 92 percent of the presidents, but only 40 percent of them say that such requirements have become more important since 1969-70, and 10 percent said they have become less important
- Interdisciplinary studies are ranked as of "great or moderate" importance by 72 percent of the presidents. The variations in responses to this question suggest that the importance of interdisciplinary studies tends to be positively related to the complexity of the institution. The range is from a low of 60 percent of the presidents of Two-Year Colleges who regard interdisciplinary studies as important to the 98 percent of presidents of Research Universities I who accord them that same level of concern. This pattern is consistent, of course, with the often-heard argument that interdisciplinary studies are practical only after students have absorbed the instruction offered in general education at the lower-division level and, even then, only in institutions that have sufficiently diverse and qualified faculty expertise to make interdisciplinary programs effective

Innovative modes of instruction. The options colleges and universities make available to students are not restricted to courses and subjects and schedules. They also come in the form of different modes of instruction. In Table 36, information about the institutional use of six learning modes are shown. The most obvious finding is that high levels of usage are reported for every mode, suggesting that, when it comes to what goes on in the classroom, there is an enormous amount of conformity in higher education. However, I should point out that the mode descriptions are very general and allow for many variations. The mere "use" of a teaching mode tells us little about the extent of its use at different institutions or, for that matter, in different parts of a single institution. As much as I, personally, would like to see evidence to the contrary, I have to concede that, on the basis of our 1978 survey, and despite the reports of their widespread availability, the actual use of the "new" technologies is probably as uneven and sporadic as it was 10 years ago.

Critics of the impersonality of large lecture classes may take some comfort in the fact that lectures to large numbers of students in a grand hall or auditorium are not as pervasive in higher education as recitation-discussion sections and seminars or, for that matter, most of the other modes of instruction. An exception is "unsupervised fieldwork, internships, and nonresident periods," which is found in only 44 percent of all institutions.

During the 1970s suggestions were made by the Carnegie Commission and Council and many others to increase the flexibility of college attendance. The intent was to break the "lockstep" of four solid years of higher education, symbolically terminated with the awarding of a degree. Reformers sought to open the campuses to students who had less than full-time to devote to their studies, to give students a greater voice in planning their own courses of studies, and to build better bridges between education and work. There are at least three indications that some of that flexibility has been created. More than two-thirds of all institutions (69 percent) now have "stopout" policies that allow any undergraduate to discontinue study for periods up to one year with readmission guaranteed (Table 37). The practice was strongly recommended by the

Table 36. Percentage of institutions using six teaching-learning modes in 1978, by Carnegie classification

	Research Universities		Doctorate-granting Institutions		Comprehensive Colleges and Universities		Liberal Arts Colleges		Two-Year Colleges	All institutions
	I	II	I	II	I	II	I	II		
Lectures to large classes	97.4%	97.3%	97.6%	94.8%	92.9%	90.9%	84.8%	72.9%	71.8%	81.6%
Recitation/discussion sections, seminars	100.0	100.0	100.0	100.0	100.0	100.0	100.0	98.1	95.9	97.8
Laboratory work	100.0	100.0	100.0	100.0	99.0	98.2	91.8	94.0	98.3	97.7
"New" technologies (CAI, PSI, video and audio tapes)	92.2	94.3	92.7	92.9	93.0	89.4	80.4	82.8	90.5	89.0
Supervised fieldwork, internships, nonresident periods	97.4	97.3	100.0	100.0	99.5	99.0	89.1	94.3	81.2	89.4
Unsupervised fieldwork, internships, nonresident periods	50.2	55.7	48.9	59.7	58.5	46.8	37.0	49.4	36.0	44.1

Source: Carnegie Council Surveys, 1978.

Table 37. Status of selected policies and programs at institutions of higher education: Percentage indicating programs were "in effect" in 1978, by Carnegie classification

| | Research Universities | | Doctorate-granting Institutions | | Comprehensive Colleges and Universities | | Liberal Arts Colleges | | Two-Year Colleges | All institutions |
	I	II	I	II	I	II	I	II		
Compensatory or remedial education (instruction in reading, writing, arithmetic, or other basic skills)	72.9%	90.9%	74.5%	75.8%	80.8%	75.9%	68.6%	72.2%	85.6%	80.6%
A "stopout" policy allowing any undergraduate to discontinue study for periods up to one year, with readmission guaranteed	70.5	75.5	66.7	71.9	68.8	65.0	84.1	59.8	71.4	68.7
An external degree program that enables students to pursue most of their education off campus and out of class	6.2	25.0	26.4	17.8	18.8	14.8	4.3	23.8	15.7	17.3

An individualized major allowing undergraduates to create their own concentration as an alternative to established majors	86.0	70.5	64.2	60.0	44.3	48.3	74.3	56.9	29.0	43.5
A cooperative educational program, alternating classroom study and off-campus work or service	52.0	62.8	58.5	60.7	61.3	44.3	21.5	40.5	56.6	52.3

Source: Carnegie Council Surveys, 1978.

Carnegie Commission on Higher Education in 1971. The range of relative frequency with which "stopout" policies are now found in higher education is from 60 percent in Liberal Arts Colleges II to 84 percent in Liberal Arts Colleges I. Resistance to this option seems greatest when an institution is small and does not have a large enough faculty to offer required courses at frequent intervals or cannot afford the luxury of forfeiting the financial security associated with dependable enrollment levels.

Another widely recommended option that permits undergraduates to create their own majors also seems to be associated strongly with comprehensiveness, since it is found most frequently at universities. The fact that it is also found at 74 percent of the Liberal Arts Colleges I suggests that individualized majors also are associated with institutions with high levels of student ability.

Programs that alternate classroom study and off-campus work or service—cooperative education—are found at 52 percent of the nation's colleges and universities but are most often found at Research Universities II, Comprehensive Universities and Colleges I, and Doctorate-granting Institutions II, in that order.

In all candor, it is difficult to demonstrate on the basis of the Carnegie Council's survey results that the "innovations" in higher education are all positively associated with enrollment increases. Even when they are—as is the case with large lecture classes at universities and the use of the new electronic technologies at two-year colleges—the correlation can be as reliably explained by institutional accommodation to more students as by student preference for certain learning modes. The content of the curriculum is what students go to a college or university to obtain, and the relationship between the subjects taught and enrollment trends is clear. But students are not as aware as they should be of the full variety of instructional modes that are available, of the different sizes and shapes of the educational packages that are offered, and of the options for flexibility that may be available. When they encounter these options on their own campuses, many of them are likely to assume that whatever they find is simply the way things are done at a college or university. Unless they attend more than one college, they may never know other modes and options exist.

Expanded Evening and Weekend Programs

There appear to be limits to what a college or university can do to entice larger shares of the finite pool of traditional students to their campuses. Altering the curriculum and providing more options in the methods of instruction can help, but, in the long run, may make only marginal differences.

Many colleges are therefore placing less emphasis on creating variety for their traditional undergraduate students and more on seeking out older students that can be served by instruction given off campus, or on evenings and weekends. It is in these efforts that I discern what may be the source of the most extensive transformation of the character of American higher education to result from the innovations of the 1970s.

Webster College in St. Louis, Missouri, is one of the institutions leading the way in these developments. On the basis of its undergraduate program, which enrolled 1,100 students in 1977, the college was classified by the Carnegie Council (1976) as a Liberal Arts College II, but it has become something different than that. In 1964, it started a Master of Arts in Teaching program designed for full-time practicing teachers. The program is now organized into seven departments, six of which are on the main campus and one of which is in Kansas City. The Master of Arts in Teaching program now has 550 students, all of whom are working teachers who attend classes at Webster College in the evenings or in the summer.

An even larger program, with 2,500 students in 1977, is Webster's Master of Arts Individualized Degree program, which offers classes for "counselors, law enforcement officers, parole officers, corporation managers, health care administrators, civil servants, and military personnel" (Webster College, 1977, p. 13). Designed primarily for working adults, the classes are organized into eight-week terms and are held mainly in the evenings and on weekends. The program is conducted on the main campus and at several off-campus locations, including about 20 military bases. When I visited the college in 1979, a branch was soon to be opened in Geneva, Switzerland. About three times as many students (on a headcount basis) are enrolled in these programs as those enrolled in regular classes on the main campus.

In many instances, the tuition of the students enrolled in programs like those offered by Webster College is paid by their employers. So the new offerings help the college to build closer relationships with companies and institutions in nearby communities. The programs may also be taught by part-time faculty members who are not in regular departments and therefore not subject to the institution's usual academic personnel policies. Such arrangements can promote administrative and fiscal flexibility.

Webster College is proud of its innovative record in higher education. It is neither the first nor the only college to offer special programs for adult students in the evenings and on weekends, or to offer, at the undergraduate level, an assessment of experiential learning, but it has gone into the venture in an ambitious and carefully planned way. A visitor cannot escape a feeling that there may be, in reality, two Websters. One is the liberal arts college that performs the institution's traditional function (heavily laced with commitments to exploit the cultural resources of St. Louis and to offer professional training in the performing arts). The other is the graduate program that currently concentrates on instruction tailored to its individualized master's degree students. I cannot help but wonder if individualized doctorates are not a possibility if the logic of these developments is pursued to the ultimate. I also wonder if institutions like Webster will remain a part of traditional higher education or become a part of a distinct new category of institutions that specialize in programs for working adults seeking degree completion programs and in relatively short-term graduate programs designed for older students that offer mainly occupational and professional curricula.

Programs similar to those of Webster College already exist in the University of LaVerne's Professional Development Centers that offer master's level work in education and management. As is the case with Webster College, the programs of the

University of LaVerne are offered at many locations. One target of their programs is the student who is older than 22 and has less than full time to give to college study.

Older students are attracted to colleges and universities that schedule programs at times that are particularly convenient for them. In 1971, Long Island University started its C. W. Post Weekend College offering courses in the liberal arts and professional fields. Its students can earn associate of arts and bachelor's degrees in weekend classes taught by members of the regular Long Island faculty (Levine, 1978, p. 242).

In its final report, *Three Thousand Futures* (1980), the Carnegie Council on Policy Studies in Higher Education presents a detailed supplement (Supplement G) on academic schedules and the split-level week. Using data from the Carnegie Surveys of 1978, it reports that 91 percent of American colleges and universities now offer at least some degree-credit courses in the evening and 40 percent offer degree-credit courses on weekends. The supplement does point out, however, that *programs* (involving more than individual courses) are less likely than courses to be offered on split-level schedules and that there are important differences between types of institutions.

According to the summary:

1. Public colleges and universities (especially two-year campuses) are more likely than private institutions to report that "one or more programs are designed so that some students may complete all (or nearly all) work for a degree by attending classes: only in the morning; only in the afternoon; only in the evening; on selected days of the week; or in the summer."
2. Equal percentages of private and public institutions offer programs that can be completed (1) only on weekends or (2) in special, intensive sessions, for example, two weeks, twice a year, plus independent study.
3. The most common "split-level scheduling option" involves the possibility of completing work for a degree in the evening. This option is available at 74 percent of the public and 38 percent of the private campuses. The least

common options in both public and private sectors involve weekend and special, intensive sessions.

4.   Among public institutions, two-year colleges are some-what more likely than four-year colleges to offer morning, afternoon, evening, and selected-days-of-the-week options, but are somewhat less likely to offer weekend, summer, and special, intensive-sessions programs.

5.   Among private institutions, two-year campuses are less likely than their four-year counterparts to offer all options except exclusively morning or afternoon schedules.

In all categories of institutions responding to the Carnegie Surveys of 1978, increases are reported in evening programs. Among the institutions responding to questions about scheduling changes, weekend programs increased at 90 percent of the pri-vate institutions and at 84 percent of the public institutions.

In the Carnegie Surveys of 1978, respondents were pre-sented with several split-level schedule options and asked "Does this statement apply now?" Those who answered "No" were asked, in part, "Are you considering or planning for this in the future?" Among the highlights of the responses, as re-ported in the Council's final report (1980) are:

1.   Public institutions are not only more likely than private ones to offer these options now but also are more likely to be considering their adoption in the future. Exceptions are summer and intensive sessions, where the proportions are equal for both public and private.

2.   The most dramatic findings are in the category of week-end programs. Now, only 8 percent of all institutions offer such programs, but 43 percent of the public and 35 percent of the private institutions that are not already offering this option are considering it for the future.

3.   Since almost three-fourths of the public institutions now offer evening programs, only a few are left to adopt this option. Yet, almost 50 percent of the public institutions (and 39 percent of the private) that do not now have

evening programs are considering starting them. Comprehensive and two-year institutions are especially likely to start such programs in the future.

4. The public Two-Year Colleges emerge as the most innovative of all categories with respect to new schedule options. In the case of every option except intensive sessions, they are the most likely of all public institutional categories to be considering adoption.

5. The private Research Universities I and Liberal Arts Colleges I that do not now offer these options plan to cling most strongly to more traditional scheduling structures. These schools may enroll higher than average numbers of more "traditional" students, and they are in the categories least likely to be affected by enrollment declines.

In addition to the five causes of enrollment increase discussed above, four others were included as options in the questionnaire used in the Carnegie Council surveys of institutional adaptations to the 1970s. They were the improvement of student services, mentioned by 48 percent of the college offices; improvement of teaching, mentioned by 40 percent; better scheduling of daytime classes, mentioned by 24 percent; and a more convenient location and better transportation, mentioned by 16 percent. Direct relationships between increased enrollments and the presence or absence of such factors are difficult to identify and measure, however. Moreover, as in the case of improved student services, these factors probably have a stronger influence on enrollment by increasing retention rather than by enlarging the pool of prospective students or attracting more students for the first time.

The Reasons for Decreasing Enrollments

When students start leaving colleges or universities—or fail to even try them—there are not always simple explanations. All students have their own reasons, and not all reasons apply to all institutions equally.

In the Carnegie Council Survey of 1978, the five factors most frequently cited as a cause of decreased full-time equivalent (FTE) enrollment by all responding college and university officials (Table 38) are:

Decline in interest in the liberal arts (64%)
End of the military draft (59%)
Increase in percentage of part-time students (59%)
High tuition (38%)
Increase in percentage of transfer students relative to freshmen (34%).

When only institutions that actually experienced enrollment decreases since 1969 are considered in Table 39, a similar listing results—but with some important differences. The decline in interest in the liberal arts continues to rank as the number one cause of enrollment decrease at public institutions but drops to second rank at private institutions. The end of the military draft drops to ninth rank at public institutions and third rank at private ones. High tuition is ranked eighth as a cause of enrollment decline at public institutions and sixth at private ones. The decline in retention rates ranks second as a cause of enrollment decrease at public colleges that lost students and first at private institutions with enrollment loss (Table 39).

A decline in interest in the liberal arts would be expected to be widely reported as a cause of enrollment decrease by liberal arts colleges, and this response is given by 73 percent of the less-selective liberal arts colleges. As a group, Liberal Arts Colleges I and II rank this factor as third in importance. The still higher ranking of this factor by all public institutions of higher education seems to be caused by the fact that the relatively numerous public comprehensive colleges and universities rank it as the primary cause of their enrollment decline. They are joined by high percentages of Doctorate-granting Universities I and Research Universities I (Tables 37, 38).

Because a high proportion of all institutions cite the declining pull of the liberal arts as a reason for losing students, what is considered disenchantment with the liberal arts may be

Table 38. Factors bringing about a decrease in FTE enrollment since 1969-70 at institutions of higher education, by percentage of institutions by Carnegie classification

	Research Universities		Doctorate-granting Institutions		Comprehensive Colleges and Universities		Liberal Arts Colleges		Two-Year Colleges	All institutions
	I	II	I	II	I	II	I	II		
Decline in interest in liberal arts	75%	69%	76%	61%	72%	70%	62%	73%	55%	64%
End of the military draft	72	60	52	59	63	58	41	35	70	59
Increase in percentage of part-time students	47	49	59	57	55	66	38	55	65	59
Tuition too high, students cannot afford	43	44	38	55	42	47	65	63	19	38
Increase in percentage of transfer students relative to freshmen	54	47	46	61	40	43	35	44	20	34
Budget or enrollment ceiling imposed or reached	43	31	34	34	25	26	19	9	31	25
Decline in retention rates	29	31	21	34	16	19	19	8	27	20
Reduction in student work	29	31	21	34	16	19	19	8	27	20
Decline in interest in innovations begun within the past 15 years at this institution	18	19	18	21	8	17	14	16	15	14

Source: Carnegie Council Surveys, 1978.

Table 39. Ranking of importance of factors bringing about decreases in enrollment at all institutions and at public and private institutions experiencing "substantial" or "some" decrease in enrollment since 1969-70, by Carnegie classification

		Public institutions				Private institutions			
	All institutions	Universities	Comprehensive Universities & Colleges	Two-Year Colleges	All public institutions	Universities	Comprehensive Universities & Colleges	Liberal Arts Colleges	Two-Year Colleges	All private institutions
Reduction in student work	8	2	9	6	6	10	5	6*	4	7
Increase in percentage of part-time students	3*	6	3	7	5	5	4	5	5	4
Increase in percentage of transfer students relative to freshmen	7*	8	8	1*	7	10	7	4*	10*	8
Decline in retention rates	1	1	4	5	2	1*	1	1*	2*	1
Decline in interest in liberal arts	2	3	1	4	1	3	2	3	1	2

Decline in interest in innovations begun within the past 15 years at this institution	3*	5	6	1*	4	6	6	4*	6	5
Budget or enrollment ceiling imposed or reached	6	7	2	1*	3	1*	10	10	10*	8
End of the military draft	5	9	5	8	9	4	3	1*	2*	3
Tuition too high, students cannot afford	7*	4	7	9	8	7	8	6*	7	6

*Ties receive identical ranking. A "zero" response is scored as 10. Ranking is scored on scale of 1-10.

Source: Carnegie Council Surveys, 1978.

translated by many respondents into the assumption that there
is public disenchantment with traditional, academic higher
education in general. It is also related to a decreasing demand
for teachers because liberal arts courses provide a substantial
part of teacher education.

The end of selective service in 1972 and increases in the
number of part-time students are both cited by 59 percent of
the officials of colleges and universities who participated in the
Carnegie Council surveys as factors in decreasing FTE enrollments. I had not fully appreciated the impact on college enrollments made by the end of the draft until I visited a small college
in an isolated rural community in the Midwest. There I was
told that, during the 1960s, the college attracted many young
men from the East Coast who took advantage of the college's
relatively low admissions requirements to acquire an educational exemption from military service. Enrollments at this
institution declined 22 percent between 1968 and 1978. At
larger institutions, however, the impact of the end of selective
service was seldom so drastic (Table 39).

The concern of colleges and universities for the consequences of increased part-time enrollments is related to the way
money and other resources are allocated to institutions. In state
funding formulas, it usually takes two or three part-time students to justify the same share of financial support that is
provided for one full-time student. Part-time enrollments tend
to dramatize declining traditional enrollments because, if full-
time enrollments had held steady or increased in recent years,
the addition of part-time students would have been considered
part of an increase, rather than a factor in enrollment decline.
There would have been a net gain instead of a net loss. Increased transfer student enrollments accompanied by decreasing
freshman enrollments also result in a net loss because transfer
students spend less time on one campus.

Although high tuition is regarded as a fairly high-ranking
cause of enrollment decrease by all institutions (Table 38), it
is not highly ranked at institutions that have actually experienced
enrollment decreases since 1969-70 (Table 39). Moreover,
it is much less frequently cited by officials of private institutions

than it is by those at public colleges and universities (Table 40). Only 2 percent of the private liberal arts colleges and 2 percent of private comprehensive universities report high tuition as a cause of either "substantial" or "some" decrease in enrollments. But it is a factor in downward enrollment trends at 33 percent of the private two-year colleges that experienced enrollment decline since 1969-70.

In the Carnegie Council Surveys of 1978, college and university presidents were asked to indicate whether they agreed or disagreed with the following statements:

"Tuition costs are already about as high as they can go at this institution."
"Tuition costs are as high as they should go at most public institutions."
"Tuition costs are as high as they should go at most private institutions."

Only 36 percent of the responding presidents agree that tuition has reached a limit at their own institutions; 40 percent agree that tuition is as high as it should go at public institutions; and 51 believe that tuition is as high as it should go at private institutions. There is general agreement among presidents of both public and private institutions on the appropriateness of current tuition levels at private institutions and at colleges and universities in general, but there is disagreement over the appropriate levels of tuition in public institutions. On this issue, 63 percent of the presidents of public institutions agree or agree strongly that tuition is as high as it should go at public colleges and universities, but only 14 percent of their private counterparts share that view (Carnegie Council Surveys, 1978).

The seventh-ranking cause of enrollment decreases, according to all respondents to the 1978 surveys, was a decline in retention rates. It was experienced at 20 percent of all colleges and universities (Table 38). This is a case where limiting respondents to officials at colleges and universities that have actually lost enrollments, as in Table 39 and 40, results in a much higher ranking. Among private institutions that actually lost enrollments, declining retention ranks as the number one

Table 40. Factors bringing about decreased enrollments at institutions experiencing declining enrollments since 1969-70, in percentages of responding institutions reporting "some" or "substantial" decrease, by Carnegie classification and control

	Public institutions			Private institutions			
	Universities	Comprehensive Universities & Colleges	Two-Year Colleges	Universities	Comprehensive Universities & Colleges	Liberal Arts Colleges	Two-Year Colleges
Reduction in student work	86%	44%	76%	0%	66%	66%	33%
Increase in percentage of part-time students	57	89	64	51	70	65	44
Increase in percentage of transfer students relative to freshmen	39	49	100	0	28	0	50
Decline in retention rates	100	82	86	100	100	94	100
Decline in interest in liberal arts	66	94	89	87	96	100	86
Decline in interest in innovations begun within the past 15 years at this institution	56	50	100	39	48	44	50
Budget or enrollment ceiling imposed or reached	44	93	100	100	0	0	0
End of the military draft	34	70	61	66	81	94	100
Tuition too high, students cannot afford	63	50	0	11	2	2	33

Source: Carnegie Council Surveys, 1978.

factor in enrollment decline; officials of public institutions that lost enrollment rank declining retention rates second to the decline in interest in the liberal arts (Table 39).

Colleges and universities themselves can do something about increasing retention rates, and many of them are actively trying to do so. When the Carnegie Council invited college and university officials to describe the changes they had made to improve retention, the final list contained more than 20 items, but only 6 are mentioned frequently enough to discuss (Carnegie Council Surveys, 1978). They are:

1. Improving advising, counseling, and orientation programs; and closely monitoring student progress. This change is mentioned by officials at 590 institutions—55 percent of those responding to the question.
2. Instituting learning centers and special instruction— mentioned by 36 percent of the institutions.
3. Making curricular changes that permit more individualized instruction and more flexible class scheduling—mentioned by 13 percent of the institutions.
4. Instituting career planning programs—mentioned by 9 percent of the institutions.
5. Conducting exit interviews and followups on dropouts— mentioned by 9 percent of the institutions.
6. Relaxing rules on student discipline and behavior and giving students more freedom on campus—mentioned by 8 percent of the institutions.

Other changes made to improve student retention rates include making admissions more selective; improving living accommodations and other campus facilities; providing better transportation to the campus; making financial aid more readily available; arranging more student-faculty contacts; allowing stopouts or leaves of absences and offering off-campus study programs; offering more services to nontraditional students; and starting a cooperative education program.

Most of the most-often-mentioned strategies for improving retention are used by all types of colleges and universities (Table 41). Certain types of institutions, however, tend not to

Table 41. Percentage of institutions of higher education reporting selected changes in policies and practices designed to enhance retention of students, by Carnegie classification, 1978

	Research Universities		Doctorate-granting Institutions		Comprehensive Colleges and Universities		Liberal Arts Colleges		Two-Year Colleges	All institutions
	I	II	I	II	I	II	I	II		
Orientation, advising, and counseling programs	61%	56%	52%	90%	70%	69%	50%	65%	9%	55%
Selective admissions	6	11	4	6	4	2	0	0	5	3
More flexible curriculum, permitting reduced load	18	6	3	0	12	10	22	15	13	13
Improved facilities	11	24	4	9	4	6	0	6	4	5
More financial aid	6	6	3	13	1	4	13	0	5	4
Relaxation of student rules	6	0	0	0	7	12	3	16	7	8
Learning centers, remedial programs, advanced placement, individualized instruction	50	44	34	34	39	38	19	17	44	36
Exit interviews, followups	11	16	7	0	6	11	16	9	8	9
More student-faculty contact provided	6	6	0	9	10	3	3	3	6	6

More service to older, part-time, minority students	11	22	4	13	2	3	0	6	2	3
Career planning programs	0	11	3	16	7	10	13	21	4	9
More grading options, changed repeat policies	0	6	11	6	1	2	0	0	6	3
Improved student activities and services	11	0	7	0	1	3	19	6	10	7

Source: Carnegie Council Surveys, 1978.

conform to prevailing practices. Liberal Arts Colleges II, for example, are twice as likely as other institutions to relax rules on student behavior, but they are somewhat more willing than other types of institutions to make curricular changes that provide more individualized instruction and more flexible class scheduling. Their smaller size apparently makes individualized instruction more feasible than it would be at more comprehensive institutions. Doctorate-granting Universities II and Comprehensive Universities and Colleges apparently are more likely than all other types of institutions to concentrate on advising and counseling programs to increase student retention.

The efforts of American colleges and universities to retain their students will make the 1980s and 1990s, in the terms of the Carnegie Council's final report, a "golden age" for students. Students will, indeed, be "retained more assiduously, counseled more attentively, graded more considerately, financed more adequately, taught more conscientiously, placed in jobs more insistently" (Carnegie Council, 1980). The curriculum will also be tailored more to their tastes and interests.

"The decline of interest in innovations begun within the past 15 years at this institution" was reported as a factor in enrollment decline by 14 percent of all college and university officials participating in the 1978 Carnegie Survey (Table 38). But this factor still ranks third in importance as a factor in enrollment decline at institutions that actually experienced a decrease in the size of their student bodies (Table 39). Unhappily, there is nothing in the survey responses that tells us precisely which innovations the college officials have in mind. Looking back over the 1970s, some of the most important innovations now found at colleges and universities are precisely those described earlier in this section as having been invoked as antidotes for dropout rates. They also include measures designed to attract more adult and more part-time students. It is difficult to believe that all of these efforts should be judged as failures. It is true also that the introduction of electronic media for instruction, the use of self-instruction techniques, and the introduction of certain other instructional innovations did not achieve the levels of success some of us predicted they might, but since these innovations were often highly experimental and were not widely employed in any event, it is difficult to envision experiences with them as having been so disastrous as to have driven significant numbers of students away from colleges and universities. Under the circumstances, it may be best to regard this response to the survey in much the same way as one might interpret the reports that a decline in interest in the liberal arts was a factor in enrollment decline. The response seems to speak more to a general impression of public disaffection with higher education in the 1970s than to specific programs.

Finally, about 25 percent of all institutions report that enrollment decreased because budget or enrollment ceilings that were set either by the institution or by coordinating agencies in the state had been reached. This cause of enrollment decrease is reported by 100 percent of the public two-year colleges, 44 percent of the public universities, and 93 percent of the public comprehensive universities and colleges (Carnegie Council Surveys, 1978). One hundred percent of the private universities but none of the private liberal arts colleges report enrollment decreases resulting from budget ceilings or other planned limitations (ibid.). Although smallness is not necessarily a virtue in higher education, some of the institutions that deliberately restricted growth in the 1960s proved to be wise. By resisting the temptation to expand too much, they avoided the painful consequences of excess capacity that some colleges and universities encountered in the 1970s.

The Competition for Students

One factor in enrollment decline that has not yet been discussed in this chapter is the increased competition among colleges and universities for the students that are available. Across the country, 89 percent of the college and university presidents responding to the Carnegie Council Surveys of 1978 report that they are experiencing increased competition. No classification of college or universities seems exempt, and no single sector is a major source of competition for all others (Table 42).

Table 42. Percentage of institutions reporting experiences with competition for students from other institutions of postsecondary education, 1978, by Carnegie classification

	Research Universities I	Research Universities II	Doctorate-granting Institutions I	Doctorate-granting Institutions II	Comprehensive Colleges and Universities I	Comprehensive Colleges and Universities II	Liberal Arts Colleges I	Liberal Arts Colleges II	Two-Year Colleges	All institutions
Campus has experienced competition for students from other postsecondary institutions—	63%	73%	86%	97%	94%	88%	87%	92%	89%	89%
From on-campus programs of four-year institutions	92	85	83	85	82	84	98	74	62	73
From off-campus programs of four-year institutions or nontraditional colleges	46	48	38	52	43	5	24	48	41	38
From two-year community or junior colleges	46	70	91	64	71	34	73	57	62	46
From public vocational-technical centers or institutions	13	15	20	26	24	30	10	26	34	28
From proprietary or other private specialty schools	13	8	8	20	11	12	5	20	26	19
From other	8	8	5	4	3	3	0	0	4	3

Source: Carnegie Council Surveys, 1978.

The competition is particularly threatening to small private institutions located in rural areas. Often, their sites were chosen many years ago when college builders believed that removing students from the temptations and perils of the big cities was essential to effective higher education. To the extent that such colleges were isolated and mainly served students of a single religious denomination, they were also protected from competition from other institutions of higher learning.

In the 1960s and 1970s, choosing a site for college campuses was determined by new considerations—the availability of a site large enough to accommodate the facilities planned, accessibility by freeways and public transportation, and proximity to metropolitan areas, for example. Moreover, much of the building was done by state and local governments and was intended to provide higher education for students of all denominations and students of moderate and low incomes as well as those from more affluent families. The consequence of such building has been to intensify the competition that probably has existed between colleges and universities ever since more than one was available.

Modern competition takes several forms—competition in geographic convenience, competition in the comprehensiveness of offerings, and competition in price. One reason why small private colleges feel competition so intensely is that they tend to be vulnerable on all counts. During our visits to colleges and universities in spring 1979, members of the Carnegie Council staff were told again and again of the threats posed to small colleges by a new community college "just 35 miles down the freeway" or by a new public four-year college opening up within the private college's historic service territory.

But the small private colleges are not the only victims. Competition involves colleges and universities of all types. The on-campus programs of other four-year institutions are regarded as competitive by 73 percent of the institutions in the country. The programs of two-year colleges are considered competitive by 46 percent.

The fact that 38 percent of all American colleges and universities now regard "off-campus programs of four-year institutions or nontraditional colleges" as a source of competition bears watching in the coming decades. Universities of all types and the Comprehensive Universities and Colleges I appear to be the most threatened by such programs. And that probably particularly reflects an awareness and concern for the expansion of graduate-level programs offered to part-time, short-term students.

Conclusion—Enrollment Decline and the New "Consumerism"

The term most frequently invoked to describe the current forces producing major changes in higher education is "consumerism." The term is hated by many writers about higher education because it seems to turn a noble enterprise into something crass and commercial. I personally do not object to the term as long as it is used to describe what I think it does—a supply and demand condition in which there are not enough people who can seek out and pay for education to take advantage of all the opportunities for higher learning that are available. They have many options open to them.

That condition clearly describes the current period in higher education. And it is also responsible for a substantial amount of the change that is taking place within higher education. The only other force of comparable importance in the dynamics of higher education in the 1970s is the effort to give greater emphasis to career outcomes as opposed to academic outcomes of education. And even that change may not have the long-term consequences that are likely to emerge from the adjustments of colleges and universities to enrollment decline.

7

Prospects

Changes Presidents Would Like to See in the 1980s

Asked to say what changes they would like to see at their institutions in the next decade, the presidents responding to the Council's 1978 surveys cast an impressively strong vote for improved quality. For example, 42 percent of them mention improved academic programs (the highest-ranked of all the goals mentioned); 29 percent want improved or expanded physical facilities; 15 percent want improvement in the quality of the faculty; and 12 percent want improvement in the overall quality of their institutions (Table 43).

The fact that the presidents of Comprehensive Colleges and Universities I are a large proportion of all presidents that want quality improvements in the next decade (Table 44) is consistent with the "follow-the-leader" theory that many of these institutions are "universities trying to happen." However, strong support for improvement of quality in all four-year colleges obviously exists, and differences between institutions of different classifications are not as significant as the general trend.

The second-ranked response to our question about desired changes for the coming decade is "increased endowment" (Table 43). If this change is combined with the tenth-ranked "improved fund raising," the desire for increased financial support from private sources would rise to the top in the ranking of desired changes. This change would mean more than more money—as attractive as that would be—because endowment and private gifts offer a special and preferred kind of

Table 43. Frequency and percentage of presidents responding to the question: "Within the next decade, what changes would you like to see at your institution?"

| | Number of mentions | | | Percentage[a] of all presidents |
	Public institutions	Private institutions	All institutions	
Improved academic programs	545	373	918	42%
Increased endowment	363	413	776	36
Improved or expanded physical facilities	331	301	632	29
Institutional goals defined	253	215	468	21
Increased enrollment	105	231	336	15
Improved faculty	141	191	332	15
Changes in administrative personnel	179	106	285	13
Improved quality of the institution	130	126	256	12
More continuing education	82	77	159	7
Improved fund raising	54	95	149	7
More institutional autonomy	106	7	113	5
More career education	51	13	64	3
Reduced influence of unions	36	2	38	2
Reduced enrollment	12	6	18	1
Other changes	198	159	357	16

[a]Percentages do not add to 100 because up to three mentions were tallied for each respondent.

Source: Carnegie Council Surveys, 1978.

funding that gives institutions discretion in spending and provides, at least in the case of an endowment, predictable levels of support. The desire for such funding is also consistent with desires for "more institutional autonomy," the eleventh-ranked change, which is mentioned nine times more often by presidents of public institutions than it is by presidents of private colleges and universities. Increased endowment is desired by presidents of private and public institutions alike.

"Institutional goals defined" is a relatively high-ranking (fourth) change (Table 44) among what one might refer to as "II-level" institutions in each of the Carnegie classifications. In almost all cases, these are the least comprehensive and least fully developed of the institutions in the five major categories. In these institutions, the presidents' desires for changes may express a sense that their institutions are in transition and may reflect their doubts as to which direction they should move. One cannot discount the very likely and more generalized possibility, however, that presidential desires for better-defined goals reflect nothing more than a general sense of institutional disorientation in the wake of rapid growth and change in the 1960s and 1970s and uncertainty about alternative courses for the future.

"Increased enrollment" ranks fifth among the desired changes (Table 44) and, as has been indicated previously, is a change associated with financial stability.

It is hard to discern specifically what "changes in administrative personnel" might turn out to be on college and university campuses. The one clear example is the male president of a women's college who lists as the first change he desires: "A woman president to take my place!" Others are less specific, but indicate that they feel responsible for the performance, competence, and compatability of their administrative colleagues.

Two changes that are desired by some of the presidents have a decidedly contemporary ring. They are "more continuing education programs" and "more career education." Continuing education appeals to college presidents as an essential component of the educational services needed by a learning society. Many institutions are also discovering that it provides

Table 44. Percentage of presidents who mentioned 15 changes in response to the question: "Within the next decade, what changes would you like to see at your institution?" (First three mentions tallied)

	Research universities		Doctorate-granting institutions		Comprehensive colleges & universities		Liberal arts colleges		Two-Year colleges	
	I	II	I	II	I	II	I	II	I	II
Improved academic programs	40%	48%	49%	42%	55%	47%	49%	37%	37%	
Increased endowment	37	52	24	49	32	32	44	41	34	
Improved or expanded physical facilities	12	35	22	18	23	24	26	40	29	
Institutional goals defined	12	22	10	22	11	24	19	26	24	
Increased enrollment	3	3	10	16	16	20	21	33	7	
Improved faculty	21	35	22	27	24	28	21	16	7	
Changes in administrative personnel	9	7	10	5	11	14	12	7	17	
Improved quality of the institution	30	23	32	24	25	18	16	11	3	
More continuing education	0	18	12	4	7	2	17	7	8	
Improved fund raising	6	0	5	7	10	10	12	4	6	
More institutional autonomy	12	3	2	11	2	4	2	0	9	
More career education	0	0	8	0	9	5	7	0	1	
Reduced influence of unions	3	3	0	0	2	2	0	0	3	
Reduced enrollment	10	0	7	0	32	22	15	0	0	
Other changes	25	10	27	25	10	11	5	18	19	

Source: Carnegie Council Surveys, 1978.

new sources of students to buttress declining enrollments. It is also related to some of the formulations of what a learning society entails. Only in Research Universities I do no presidents mention it as a desired goal. Continuing education probably is not attractive to research and doctorate-granting institutions because many of their resources are committed to training students for careers in academic life. It *is* attractive, however, to comprehensive colleges and universities because, by definition, they already provide instruction in occupational and professional departments and divisions.

Taken altogether, the presidents' desired changes give us reason for optimism. Although additional state funds or bigger budgets are mentioned by a few individual presidents, the changes most preferred are those that will improve the quality of colleges and universities, increase their independence, and render them of service to broader segments of society.

Issues for the 1980s and 1990s

The final question in the Carnegie Council's 1978 survey of college and university presidents was: "In your judgment, what are likely to be the most important issues facing American higher education between 1980 and the year 2000?" In all, perhaps 60 to 70 issues were identified, ranging from the almost cosmic "redefining the goals of higher education" to such specific concerns as "remedial education" and "faculty salaries."

I will concentrate on the 10 most frequently mentiond issues, ranging from "financing higher education," which was mentioned by 1,210 presidents (55 percent) to "continuing education," which was mentioned by 163 presidents (7 percent) (Table 45). Institutional variations on these issues are summarized in Table 46.

In descending order of the frequency with which they were mentioned, the 10 issues are:

1. Financing higher education
2. Redefining the goals of higher education
3. Maintaining enrollments
4. Maintaining the autonomy of higher education

Table 45. Frequency and percentage of presidents giving the 10 most frequent responses to the question: "What are likely to be the most important issues facing American higher education between 1980 and the year 2000?"

Responses	Number of mentions			Percentage[a] of all presidents
	Public institutions	Private institutions	All institutions	
Financing higher education	697	513	1,210	54%
Redefining goals of higher education	591	274	865	39
Maintaining enrollments	362	330	692	31
Maintaining autonomy of higher education	266	265	531	24
Strengthening liberal arts	212	236	448	20
Preserving private sector	80	336	416	19
Maintaining quality in higher education	163	183	346	15
Strengthening career education	195	84	278	13
Public confidence in higher education	173	60	233	11
Continuing education	105	58	163	7

[a]Percentages do not add to 100 because up to three mentions were tabulated, and only 10 of 22 tabulated responses are shown.
Source: Carnegie Council Surveys, 1978.

Table 46. Percentage of presidents giving the 10 most frequent answers to the question:
"What are likely to be the most important issues facing American higher education between 1980 and the year 2000?"
(First three mentions tallied)

	Research universities		Doctorate-granting institutions		Comprehensive colleges & universities		Liberal arts colleges		Two-Year colleges
	I	II	I	II	I	II	I	II	
Financing higher education	57%	56%	67%	46%	50%	55%	73%	45%	56%
Redefining goals of higher education	25	24	28	47	33	35	29	29	48
Maintaining enrollments	31	33	39	40	41	36	40	29	25
Maintaining autonomy of higher education	30	30	17	13	27	22	18	23	24
Strengthening the liberal arts	13	17	24	24	23	36	31	22	14
Preserving private sector	23	18	19	24	13	21	40	35	11
Maintaining quality in higher education	23	16	26	11	12	22	20	21	12
Strengthening career education	0	0	0	4	12	9	2	14	16
Public confidence in higher education	6	10	19	9	18	6	7	5	11
Continuing education	0	10	8	0	6	4	2	7	10

Source: Carnegie Council Surveys, 1978.

5. Strengthening the liberal arts
6. Preserving the private sector
7. Maintaining quality in higher education
8. Strengthening career education
9. Public confidence in higher education
10. Continuing education.

Financing higher education. This issue is frequently cast in the form of a question: "Who will pay for higher education?" or "How to pay the costs of the services required?" or, in more detail, "What is the appropriate amount of state and federal support for higher education? To what extent can public funding formulae differentiate between colleges and research universities, and between graduate and undergraduate education?" In other instances, it is cast in a statement of some part of the problem: "The financial issues are especially related to enrollment and the tuition gap between public and private and fund raising for the latter." Or it is cast in a conception of the ultimate solution: "Willingness of society to invest substantially in higher education." However it is phrased, it becomes essentially the same thing: uncertainty about where the money is coming from to finance higher education in the future and the need for rationales with which colleges and universities can argue for their appropriate share of support from both the public and private sectors.

Redefining the goals of higher education. Usually, this response is rather flatly stated. But there are a few elaborations worth noting, such as "redefinition . . . of the educated person," "Who will receive a college education and for what reason?" and "Does higher education have a role in nurturing moral and ethical values?" In one case the argument for goals and planning is stated basically in terms of the need for higher education to define its goals and set its course before the state or "society" does.

Maintaining enrollments. There is nothing particularly complicated about the nature of this issue, whether it is spoken of in terms of the "steady state" or just "declining enrollments." (Such cryptic responses predominate here.) The nub of the issue seems to be simply how public institutions can rationalize their need for additional funding as the number of their students goes down, and where the private institutions will find the money to make up the lost tuition of students who don't show up to enroll. Almost never mentioned as part of the issue is whether there is too much competition for students—in effect, too many institutions for the students that are available.

Maintaining the autonomy of higher education. This is usually stated in terms of "encroachment" of both federal and state governments, although accrediting agencies are occasionally mentioned. One frequently mentioned concern is the possiblity that government regulations will make "most institutions of higher education 'uniform'." One president puts the dilemma succinctly: "How to keep the independence of the university even though we need outside support."

Strengthening the liberal arts. This issue is frequently raised in terms of the threat to liberal arts posed by vocational and career education. One president says: "My particular concern is that the institutions of higher learning struggle valiantly to maintain the liberal arts and science/cultural objectives. The rising tide of careerism is symptomatic of the overwhelming urge of Americans to defer to Babbitry." But the issue is also stated as an assertion of a need to find "imaginative ways to use liberal arts in significant new programs" or to find the best of both worlds by "effecting a viable 'marriage' between general education (liberal arts) and career preparation."

Preserving the private sector. One president may have said it all: "The single most important question facing American higher education is whether or not the nation is going to be willing to pay for a dualistic system of higher education without discriminating against independent colleges and universities. If the nation does not decide to pay for such a system, it seems we shall end up with a single monolithic state system which will, in turn, bring about a much different system of higher education that we now know."

Maintaining quality in higher education. There is fear of a "reduction of standards to keep students" and a "society unwittingly intent on doing in its major universities." A two-year college president asks: "How much quality can we afford?" The president of a private institution in Texas says: "In view of the levelling of influences that prevails today, can any degree of intellectualism be expected in the 1980s on the part of those who are now in the elementary and secondary ranks? Or will there be a compartmentalism in higher education with one section reserved for or utilized by those who are mentally superior or more highly motivated?"

Strengthening career education. The strongest argument for career education comes from the president of a small liberal arts college, who says: "Higher education must be preparation for career and life. As such, it must include more than knowledge. It must include practical application of that knowledge and must include values and purpose in life. Higher education today is woefully lacking in true preparation of our young people." The career issue as seen by many presidents is really the issue of career versus liberal education and is often stated in those terms.

Public confidence in higher education. Presidents tend to speak of public support in tandem with the need for money—"generation of sufficient public support and resources," "public image, and therefore funding." One president assesses the problem this way: "In my judgment, higher education has lost some of the priority it has enjoyed in this country for the past two hundred years. Being beleaguered by various demands, the citizens are less inclined to provide the support that is needed to maintain quality education in the numerous public and private institutions."

Continuing education. Although less than 10 percent of the presidents in our survey say this will be an issue in the 1980s and 1990s, those who do put the issue in interesting terms: "What's to be done with a changing person?" They also see the older student and continuing education as a source of hope for higher education: "Schools will either adjust to a steady state or react to new needs which are likely to be among the 25 to 50-year-old population desiring to finish college but no longer mobile. Colleges will have to reach out to these students through innovative and well-designed . . . programs—

the 1990s, I believe, will once again be a growth period for higher education."

The presidents' agenda for the coming decades is not an easy one. The issues are tough and often overlap or conflict. Some may disappear or take new forms as strategies for coping with the problems they pose are adopted and tested. But they are real, and much of the future of higher education will be determined by how they are resolved.

Forks in the Road

The future of higher education depends in part on choices that have already been made by higher education decision makers. Some of them go a long way toward solving current problems, but others have long-term consequences that merit second thoughts. In choosing the forks in the road to explore here, I have not assumed that any of them will necessarily be chosen by all kinds of institutions or even by most institutions of any one kind. Moreover, I am not trying to predict the future. I am only speculating on possible consequences if the roads are traveled too far by too many institutions without concern for where they could lead.

The continuing increase in emphasis on specialization, particularly in career fields. Some colleges and universities obviously are well along this fork of the road and for good reasons. Specialization can be a valuable part of one's education and much can be said for making the relationship between education and careers more explicit than it has been in the past. Moreover, the old-fashioned tendency to hold general, "academic" learning to be somehow more refined and valuable than specialized, utilitarian learning has little to commend it beyond an appropriate insistence that purely intellectual endeavors are not necessarily idle or useless.

However, my fear is that, if the emphasis on career preparation in colleges and universities is carried too far, too many college resources for what is often referred to as "liberal learning" will be jettisoned along the way to make room for career preparation programs. The finite dimensions of degree requirements make such decisions almost inevitable. Some of the colleges pursuing the road toward more vocational and occupational emphases have already cast off language instruction and other components of general education to make room for specialized, career-related offerings. Some of them are already reallocating the vacancies that will occur as the faculty of "low-demand" humanities departments retire or die to pre-professional or specialized departments.

The problem with all of this is that it rests on an assumption that the current, or even a greater, emphasis on specialization and career preparation is indefinitely appropriate and that a withering of general education is inevitable, perhaps overdue, and unlamented. It is very likely, however, that, once colleges and universities tool up for more specialized, career-oriented programs, a need for equilibrium between the new and the more general offerings will become increasingly apparent. The resources for offering general learning programs that are being jettisoned now will then be needed again. But they will be difficult to obtain if the faculties and facilities needed to educate the generalists of the future are not maintained at an adequate level.

The continuing trend toward comprehensiveness. Similar considerations relate to the tendency of small colleges to add functions and programs that change their basic mission and character. As I noted earlier in this study, the threat to America's liberal arts colleges is not just impending bankruptcy and failure. They are also threatened by a loss of their distinctive character and function as they become larger and more comprehensive.

It is perhaps too easy to complain about such shifts when one is not personally confronted with the hard choices that have to be made to keep a college solvent. On balance, it is surely better that an effectively functioning college accept new functions than disappear. But the consequences of losing institutions with the mission and style of good, small, liberal arts colleges are unappealing, at least to me, both from the standpoint of lost diversity in the national resources for higher learning and from the vantage point of the many students who thrive best in small, residential, college settings.

The development of new graduate-level, part-time, indi-vidualized programs. It is good to know that colleges and universities are able to respond quickly to the unmet learning needs of American society. The specialized graduate programs that are now being designed and offered for part-time, usually full-employed, students seeking specialized training in work-related fields are a case in point. They not only meet a clear need but also have provided the means for some institutions to increase both enrollments and revenues.

Before this road is traveled by too many institutions, however, some consequences for the totality of higher educa-tion should be considered. The first of these concerns the character of the degrees offered in these programs. Although many of these offerings involve studies in the evenings or on weekends for less than six months, the degrees certifying their completion are often variants of traditional academic degrees—master's degrees in general studies, master's degrees in inde-pendent studies, or master's degrees in liberal studies, for example. Some institutions offering these programs are con-sidering offering doctorates in similar formats. This is credential-ism with a vengeance.

Obviously, degrees that carry traditional academic names are more appealing to prospective students than forms of certification that have different connotations. It is regrettable, however, that the already confusing array of academic degrees must be rendered even more perplexing by the subtle variations chosen for the new degree additions. It is also regrettable that pejorative distinctions may ultimately be made between degrees that carry essentially the same names but are awarded for different amounts and kinds of study. This problem deserves the attention of regional accrediting associations throughout the country.

A second consequence is that the profitable programs for older, part-time, employed learners may in time drive out the less profitable traditional programs of private liberal arts colleges.

A third concern is that the character of the academic profession gradually may be altered as colleges and universities offer more and more programs that rely heavily on adjunct, part-time instructors. The experience of some institutions is that the approach professors take toward instruction in the traditional undergraduate classroom is inappropriate and unappreciated by predominantly older students who are professionals or experienced specialists first and students second. So they hire faculty for these programs from the community at large instead of from the academic ranks of the regular faculty. If these part-time programs expand, what the creation of essentially dual faculties at American colleges and universities will do to appointment, tenure, promotion, and sabbatical policies, not to mention collective bargaining for faculty, remains to be seen.

The changing mission of community colleges. America's community colleges are still seeking their basic mission. Originally conceived as institutions that could introduce young men and women to the general learning offered by colleges and universities in the first two years of instruction, they gradually acquired additional functions. They became institutions for the education of men and women for certain vocations and occupations and afforded a second chance to students who were unprepared for college or university at the end of their high school studies.

More recently, they have become the colleges that produce education on demand in response to the needs and wishes of the communities they serve. Not all community colleges have taken this route; many of them still specialize in vocational and technical studies, and some remain dedicated to general studies. But much of the recent growth of community colleges has been caused by their willingness to reach out to the needs of nontraditional students—older persons, part-time students, members of racial minorities, and persons seeking instruction in subjects not found at most four-year colleges and universities. On balance, one would have to judge these developments as positive ones, in the sense that they provide expanded educational opportunities for American learners.

The troublesome aspect of the development of these institutions is that their missions have become increasingly difficult to discern. And related to that problem is the possibility that the original functions of these colleges may, in the future, be deemphasized or even disappear.

The loss might not be disastrous. The new programs of these colleges do fill a need and make a legitimate claim on community resources for postsecondary education. Moreover, the expansion of an increasing number of comprehensive state colleges and universities throughout the country has made relatively low-cost education available to many students who once could have obtained it only at two-year community colleges. Thus, if all community colleges were to abandon their academic programs, there probably are institutions around that could take up the slack.

The greatest problem posed by that possibility would be faced by students who need special help in overcoming educational deficiencies that were not removed during their high school years. Community colleges have been particularly concerned about such students and have made significant efforts to help them prepare for advanced learning in colleges or universities. In the absence of two-year transfer programs at community colleges and without the compensatory or remedial education that is also available at such institutions, many students who have been especially dependent on community colleges may be stranded.

The threat to liberal arts. It is likely that the most threatened part of higher education in the United States in the 1980s and 1990s will be that part that is concerned primarily with liberal education. It is threatened, on the one hand, by the loss of institutions that have been traditionally committed to the mission of advancing the liberal arts, and, on the other hand, by the competition of new programs that draw time, attention, and resources away from traditional liberal arts programs. Liberal education may be threatened also by the distractions of community service demands made on the country's public two-year colleges.

In the years ahead, the United States may encounter an increasing need for low-cost colleges that:

1. Remain basically committed to general education in the arts and sciences as a preparation for creative, effective

participation in the society and as an undergirding for professional and occupational specialization

2.   Can help students shift from one subject field to another when they have second thoughts about educational and career objectives

3.   Can serve as a point of reentry to traditional higher education for persons who have been away from it for a long time or who seek to come back to it for studies in a subject field new to them

4.   Can provide intermediate studies for especially talented and dedicated young people of high school age who are ready for bigger challenges and a level of progress that their schools cannot give them

5.   Can provide help for students who need to acquire basic learning skills before embarking on traditional college-level studies.

All of these function have been served in the past by a variety of colleges and universities as a part of their total offerings. It now appears that the time is right to develop more "middle" colleges or "transition" colleges to perform these functions in a coordinated way. Ideally, the level of instruction offered should include that found in the last two years of high school and the first two years in college, although students would not necessarily pursue all four years of studies there.

This idea is not new. It has been proposed before, and the Carnegie Commission on Higher Education (1973) urged that it be given serious consideration. Moreover, some institutions already have experimented with programs that combine at least the first year of college with the last year or two of high school, or enroll students simultaneously in high school and in college. But such experimentation has not been extensive. Often it is thwarted by state legislation that is designed either to protect high school enrollments or the four-year programs of traditional colleges. What makes the idea timely now is that certain functions of higher education are in danger of going unserved or disserved in the future if some of the current trends in higher education continue, and the only way to protect them is to pull them together for development by special types of institutions.

It is not obvious that, at least in the immediate future, any new institutions would have to be built to make such institutions possible. Some of them could be developed by using the facilities and resources of academically oriented two-year colleges and small, academically oriented four-year colleges. In some states it also might make sense for the state government to enter contracts with small, liberal arts colleges to provide some of the services that might be rendered by middle colleges. Some private colleges also might find that an imaginative approach to the functions envisioned for middle colleges would be as attractive to students as some of the other outreach programs they have recently introduced. It would be sad, however, if the functions contemplated for middle colleges were simply incorporated as "add-ons" to any institution. To be effective, they should be carefully coordinated and should in themselves define the institution's mission, curriculum, and programs.

Strategies for the 1980s and 1990s

In its final report, the Carnegie Council on Policy Studies in Higher Education (1980) stressed that there are almost no policies for meeting the conditions of the 1980s and 1990s that are appropriate for every institution. Each institution has its own mission, its own strengths and weaknesses, its own clienteles, and its own circumstances. Each will have to chart its own course through the next two decades.

The Council report (1980, pp. 130-131) did contain a "checklist of imperatives" for colleges and universities which, while allowing for individual situations, provide broad approaches for adapting to conditions of the next two decades.

1. *Analyze All Factors Likely to Affect Future Enrollments*
   Demography ● Changing population mix ● Labor market changes ● Type of institution ● State population and fiscal trends

2. *Insist on Institutionwide or Systemwide Planning*
    Anticipate future problems ● Avoid moving from crisis to crisis ● Consider prospects for each campus in multi-campus institutions

3. *Encourage Strong Leadership by Chief Executive Officer*
    (See discussion of this subject in Chapter 3)

4. *Intensify Recruitment Efforts and Reduce Attrition*
    Rely on methods appropriate to academic life ● Avoid deceptive advertising

5. *Give High Priority to Maintenance of Quality*
    Maintain high standards for faculty ● Insist on quality in teaching ● Maintain distinctive characteristics of institutions ● Protect the internal life of the institution (discussed in Section 6 of *Three Thousand Futures*) ● Improve achievement capacity of graduates ● Emphasize high standards of scholarship—and of research in research-oriented institutions ● Preserve institutional integrity

6. *Encourage Innovation and Flexibility*
    Develop curriculum that is sensitive to change but also to emphasis on general education ● Establish fund for innovation ● Avoid too high a proportion of tenured-in faculty ● Encourage new programs and instructional techniques

7. *Strive for Most Effective Use of Resources*
    Avoid excessive number of courses and proliferation of degrees ● Review student-faculty ratios by department ● Maintain adequate support personnel ● Avoid excessive cuts in plant maintenance and library acquisitions

8. *Seek Support from Private Sources of Funds*
    Devise imaginative ways of approaching alumni and other donors

9. *Concentrate on proposals to federal and state governments that will result in better programs at no increase in the real levels of federal and state expenditures; that acknowledge the likelihood of some reductions but not proportionately to reduced enrollments.*

Beyond these general approaches, some strategies can be suggested for certain types of institutions.

Universities

The universities have a special stake in three aspects of the new conditions that confront higher education. These are the need for sustained support of research, the projected surfeit of Ph.D. programs, and the training of teachers.

Maintaining support for research. The line between a professor's teaching and research functions is often vague and imperfectly drawn. To some extent this ambiguity has benefited research activity in the past because the new positions and new facilities needed to advance research at American universities have been partially financed out of funding for instruction that increased along with growing enrollments. Now that enrollments are declining, some of that funding will be reduced or even disappear. The result is a decline in support for research and graduate studies, particularly in universities that are not heavily involved in federal support of academic science. Part of the answer is for universities to seek more direct support for research from government sources, and there are indications that, after relaxing its effort in this area for several years, the federal government, at least, is beginning to direct more funding to university-based research programs. The Carnegie Council has recommended that federal spending for research return to the same proportions of the Gross National Product (GNP) that prevailed in the 1960s.

In the long run, more than that is needed, however. If support for research is to remain stable while enrollments go up and down, state legislators, educational policy makers, and the general public will have to become much better informed than they now are about the importance of such activity to the general intellectual health and productive capacity of our country. This may require a public relations effort of massive proportions. But the stakes are great and important and deserve the concerted efforts not only of research universities, but also of national agencies and societies concerned with the advancement of scientific and intellectual endeavors.

Reducing the oversupply of doctorate holders. New Ph.D.'s confront a dismaying array of circumstances that may adversely affect their careers in higher education. Because enrollments are going down, there are fewer positions open to them—particularly in such low-demand fields as the humanities, physics, and mathematics. Because higher percentages of the faculties of colleges and universities hold tenure (in some cases entire departments are "tenured-in"), there are fewer openings made available each year for the interinstitutional transfer of young scholar-teachers. Because many colleges are staffing programs for older and part-time students with part-time, adjunct faculty members, the addition of the "new" and "nontraditional" students that are the hope of some institutions affords scant hope for the new academics.

In a planned society, it would be easy enough to simply set quotas on the number of persons to be admitted to candidacy for doctorates and raise the standards that must be met by candidates who succeed in earning these degrees and qualify for faculty membership. In a society such as our own, however, it is quite proper to ask who has the right to restrain the ambition of anyone who has the ability, desire, and determination to prepare themselves for academic careers? What is least humane? Preparing people, at great cost to themselves, to institutions, and society, for positions that may not exist? Or denying people opportunities to make the most of their talents and capacities? The resolution of that question involves the quality of the education and experience different institutions provide, the reasons why they make the effort, and the integrity with which they select the students for their advanced programs. Discussion of these matters quickly becomes a sermon everyone has heard before. The message, as tired as it is, is that, to be entirely fair, institutions will have to restrain some of their own ambitions—particularly when they lack resources of a quality that make it possible to offer future academics doctorate programs that are of truly superior caliber.

It is simply a matter of self-interest, moreover, for institutions to resist introducing new Ph.D. programs in fields in which the prognosis for future employment of successful candidates is dim. Any institution with marginal-quality programs in such fields should not hesitate to drop them. I also find appealing the idea that doctorate-granting institutions that are already

heavily engaged in research and possess strong doctorate programs in a substantial number of high-demand fields should
resist the temptation to introduce degree programs at that level
in low-cost, low-demand fields. They can thus avoid contributing to the oversupply of the Ph.D.'s. Also, until the 1990s
when enrollments begin to increase again, there is something
to be said for contributing to the general health of American
higher education by avoiding unnecessary competition with
low-cost, low-demand programs that already exist and are of
good quality at other institutions.

Contributing to the education of teachers. It may seem
paradoxical to urge universities to give even more consideration
than many of them now do to the education of teachers when
the demand for teachers is going down. It is difficult, however,
to justify the barrages of criticism of American secondary
schools originating within higher education when universities
and, to some extent, colleges have a substantial share of the
responsibility for training the teachers who work in the schools
and the administrators who run them. Perhaps there has been
no time in the history of education when a more serious concern for education at the elementary and secondary school
level on the part of faculties and leaders of our universities has
been more appropriate than it is right now. Declining school
enrollments make some of the problems of the schools slightly
more tractable, but public tolerance for the inadequacies of the
schools may be coming to an end as criticism becomes more
frequent and more widespread. Educational agencies and organizations throughout the country are beginning to mobilize to
"do something about the schools."

Part of the job of educators in colleges and universities
will be to find out what the schools are doing right. After all,
the schools prepare the students who get *A*s; write imaginative,
technically accurate, and grammatically correct term papers;
and eventually earn advanced degrees—along with the students
who drop out, enter college ill-prepared, or become problems
for the general society. What we need to learn is how to educate
more students so that they will be "successful," not only in
ways that are admired by academics, but also in ways that are

recognized in the workplace, in the home, and in the community. And when we learn how that is done, we have to find ways to make the benefits available to larger proportions of young people than we have succeeded in reaching in the past.

A nagging possibility is that there is no "one way," even in the case of preparing young people for academic life, and we may be wasting the talents of many young people by giving up on them when they fail to flourish under conditions and instruction that have, in the past, seemed adequate for "most" people. If we already know enough about the differences in learning styles found among boys and girls, we have failed to communicate what we know to either the public or the educational leaders in the country. It is amazing how educators anticipate that important educational changes will take place in the classrooms because more students will be members of ethnic minorities, more will come from a certain socioeconomic background, or more will have had parents who are college-educated. There is an assumption that these changing mixes call for different strategies for instruction, yet the relationship between these characteristics and the learning ability or style of individual students is seldom defined. Some of the characteristics could prove to be, on the whole, neutral in determining how people should be taught. What could make a real difference, however, is the mix of students who are fast or slow learners; who learn best by reading, by listening, or by repeating; who deal best with abstractions or who are most comfortable with the concrete; who are intrigued by relationships or are best at understanding components within relationships. Universities, it seems to me, have a special role as the centers of research in higher education to study the differences in learning styles and abilities among individuals and to make the results of their studies available to practicing teachers. Improving the skills of precollege students could be an important investment in the quality of college and university education in the coming decades.

Comprehensive Universities and Colleges

Many of these institutions are former teachers' colleges and continue to serve a teacher-training function. They, too, should be working with elementary and secondary schools for the improvement of learning skills of American youth.

One possibility is that some of these institutions will over-react to the decreasing need for schoolteachers during the next 15 years. Although some reduction in teacher-training activities is clearly in order, widespread abandonment of such programs would be ill-advised. A preferable strategy would be to use the 1980s and 1990s to concentrate on the improvement of the quality of teacher education and to train specialists in the instruction of students with exceptional learning styles or problems.

If the liberal arts become less important in the curricula of both the liberal arts colleges and two-year colleges—and this is a possible danger in at least some of these institutions in the coming decades—comprehensive universities and colleges will also have a responsibility to take up the slack in these subjects. In fact, because of their comprehensiveness and their broad distribution across the country, it is likely that these institutions will increasingly become the dominant centers of undergraduate education of the kind that is most familiar to the American public. Numerically, they already hold that position, and there seems to be no compelling reason for them to choose to abandon it in terms of programs and style.

At a time when the fortunes of doctorate-granting institutions with limited graduate programs and modest research activities are not too bright, it is doubtful that too many of these institutions will strive to join the comprehensive institutions during the next two decades. Some of them may be tempted, however, to provide their regional constituencies with some of the community services that are now rendered by two-year institutions. The degree to which that will turn out to be either necessary or desirable will depend on how far the public two-year colleges themselves go in that direction.

Responsible planning for these institutions might also involve the reduction or reallocation of programs and, in a few instances, the temporary phasing out of small campuses with less than the critical mass of students needed to be truly effective. It is disturbing to learn that, in some parts of the country, small, private, long-established liberal arts colleges may need 100 or fewer students to remain viable, yet find themselves in competition with public institutions that are either too isolated or too limited in their offerings to operate efficiently. Where such situations exist, consideration might be given to temporarily merging public and private institutions or temporarily dedicating marginal public campuses to specialized functions—for example, the training of paraprofessionals—that do not duplicate those of existing private liberal arts colleges. Such actions would be prudent management and not just public charity.

In a way, this suggestion may sound contradictory to the one that comprehensive institutions should be prepared to take up the function of liberal arts instruction wherever it is abandoned by two-year colleges and four-year liberal arts institutions. But, in some instances, avoiding duplication could make it unnecessary for liberal arts colleges that are threatened by competition to abandon or deemphasize their traditional functions.

Liberal Arts Colleges

It would be too bad if the reduced enrollments and resources of the 1980s and 1990s resulted in a significant loss of liberal arts colleges. Although some of their functions can be absorbed by other types of institutions, the liberal arts cannot be served in the special way that is possible when they are virtually the exclusive concern of an institution. It is for this reason that the conversion of liberal arts institutions into comprehensive institutions or into institutions primarily engaged in vocational and occupational programs for adults is saddening.

For some institutions, however, there is no alternative to such expansion and redirection. And, for a few, the circumstances of location and the availability of specialized resources make such expansion desirable and virtually inevitable.

Preferable strategies for most liberal arts colleges in the next decades are those with which most of them are all too familiar—conserving resources and recruiting as vigorously as possible. A few of them may be able to make alliances with other institutions to reduce expenses and share facilities.

Some of them may be able to identify certain programs that merit special development and marketing. An exceptional program in the performing arts is one example—although this is one subject area that seems to be ubiquitous in institutions of this type. But exceptional programs in regional history or economics, in regional literature, or other such specialties could serve to give an institution a special distinction as well as to attract students. Programs for the handicapped or for other special students could serve a similar function. It is unreasonable to expect these suggestions to save liberal arts colleges that are in desperate trouble, but they can help those that are basically sound to escape disaster.

Two-Year Colleges

These are, in many ways, America's most adaptive educational institutions, and it is this characteristic that makes them especially valuable when enrollments are declining and resources are becoming less plentiful. They can test the water when new opportunities for providing higher education arise. They can provide educational opportunities for unserved learners in a community. They can serve needs that are purely local in scope and importance. Yet they can rather easily shed functions for which there is no strong demand. Above all, unless they are horribly mismanaged, they can survive, because their functions are so numerous and their constituencies so broad and loyal that permitting them to fail is unthinkable.

Because survival is not a real problem for most of these institutions, the help they are most likely to need, not just in the 1980s and 1990s, but in the longer-term future is in defining their role in higher education. Virtually all of their present functions are now shared with other institutions. Their vocational and occupational programs can also be found at four-year comprehensive colleges and universities, at proprietary vocational and technical schools, and, to some extent, at secondary schools. Their liberal arts transfer programs are found at all four-year institutions. Some of their recreational and community service programs also are now being offered by comprehensive universities and colleges and in the adult divisions of some high schools. Their most nearly unique function, when all is said and done, is to provide educational opportunities for those who, for various reasons, have been unable to gain admission into other four-year institutions or who do not want to attend college too far away from home.

One new function recently suggested for community colleges (Carnegie Council, 1980) is that of assuming residual responsibility for the youth in their communities. This would involve "being available to all youths in the community to advise on academic and occupational opportunities, to offer job preparation classes, to make job placements, to work out individual combinations of employment and classroom instruction, to develop and to make referrals to CETA employers, to make referrals to courses of legal and medical advice, to refer and to create apprenticeship programs." This is a totally new concept and it remains to be seen whether it will be taken seriously. If it is, the United States may go further than any other industrialized country in institutionalizing its concern for giving youth a more productive role in society.

Concluding Observation

Too much of the discussion of the impending 20 years is phrased in terms of success and failure. In the preceding pages, I have, indeed, used those words myself—not so much by way of prediction as by way of suggesting that neither extreme represents the inevitable reality for most American colleges and universities in the 1980s and 1990s. Some will succeed, and some will fail—depending upon whatever definition one wishes to use for those alternatives. But, when the next two decades become a subject of history rather than conjecture, the interesting story is not likely to be about the institutions that achieved the one condition and avoided the other, but about how their efforts along the way made a difference in the overall quality and character of higher education in the United States.

Appendix A

Carnegie Council Surveys, 1978

The Carnegie Council on Policy Studies in Higher Education has made an extensive and continuous effort to keep in touch with developments on the nation's campuses. As a part of that effort, it has sponsored or conducted a series of special studies. The latest of these are the Carnegie Council's Surveys of Institutional Adaptations to the 1970s conducted in 1978.

In all, administrators of 870 American colleges and universities were invited to answer the questionnaires. The questionnaire directed to college and university presidents (Questionnaire A) was concerned with general trends, changes in control, internal governance, collective bargaining, and relationships with the outside community and with state and federal governments. The questionnaire also asked for the presidents' generalized perceptions of the most important positive and negative changes at their institutions during the past decade and their views of the major issues that higher education will face between now and the end of this century. To provide a different perspective on the matters reported by student affairs officers, presidents also were queried about student attitudes and asked to describe college students in the late 1970s.

The questionnaire directed to vice presidents of financial affairs or planning officers (Questionnaire B) explored the impact of changes in enrollment on faculty and student recruiting; personnel and tenure policies; admissions, guidance, and retention policies; selectivity; curriculum; scheduling and location; student/faculty ratios; use of available funds and student aid funds.

The questionnaire directed to student affairs officers (Questionnaire C) sought information about how undergraduates had changed and how institutions had responded to these changes; how students were involved in governing themselves and their institutions; what they were interested in (as revealed by their participation in various clubs and activities); how and what they protested. To provide perspective on the information supplied by planning officers, questions on retention policy and curriculum flexibility also were asked. The questionnaires were printed and first mailed at the end of March 1978.

From *A Classification of Institutions of Higher Education: Revised Edition* (1976), a classification of 3,072 campuses of higher education listed by the U.S. Office of Education, the staff rejected (1) all specialized and nontraditional institutions, (2) all religious schools training clergy only for religious functions, and (3) all schools not located in the 50 states or the District of Columbia. The remaining 2,481 campuses, divided by the *Carnegie Classification of Institutions of Higher Education* (1976) into 17 control (public and private) and classification categories, constituted the study universe. Seeking information from at least 30 campuses in each Carnegie classification and control category and assuming a 50 percent response rate, the staff chose at least 60 campuses from each Carnegie classification and control category for the sample. In each category with fewer than 60 campuses in the universe, every campus in the universe was chosen. This was the case for Research Universities I and II, Doctorate-granting Universities I and II, and public Liberal Arts Colleges II. Left with 2,313 campuses in other categories from which to draw our sample, the staff decided to use 120 campuses in the largest category (public Two-Year Colleges and Institutes) because of an anticipated low response rate among these institutions. The size of the sample in all remaining categories with between 60 and 909 campuses in the universe was determined by extrapolation, using a table of random numbers to select the first campus and then every third, fifth, or whatever. The resulting "original sample" contained 799 institutions. Five pretest institutions were eliminated, and the sample was adjusted in other minor ways until it stood at 794 campuses.

Questionnaires were mailed in March 1978 to liaison officers at institutions whose presidents had agreed to participate in the survey. In April it was determined that an insufficient number of postcard responses was being received in three categories: private Comprehensive Universities and Colleges I, public Comprehensive Universities and Colleges II, and private Comprehensive Universities and Colleges II. By adding 20, 28, and 28 campuses respectively to these control categories in the "original sample," the sample was increased to 870 campuses.[1]

The achieved response rate,[2] that is, the proportion of institutions eligible and able to participate in our study and choosing to do so (before the cutoff date), was 68.7 percent for complete and partial respondents; 66.9 percent for Questionnaire A; 67.6 percent for Questionnaire B; and 68.1 percent for Questionnaire C.

Response rates for each questionnaire varied only slightly because 95 percent of the institutions returning at least one questionnaire returned full sets of three questionnaires. However, response rate by Carnegie type and control shows some range (Table A-1), from 47.1 percent for private Two-Year Colleges (sample number = 71) to 94.7 percent for private Doctorate-granting Universities I (sample number = 19). Still, the variation is not great; except for private two-year colleges, Carnegie control and classification types returned questionnaires at a rate of close to 60 percent or higher, and the average rate of return (exclusive of private Two-Year Colleges) was 74.9 percent. With a response rate of 47.1 percent, private

[1]Questionnaires also were sent to and received from 130 additional women's and black institutions, but their responses were not included in basic tabulations (unless otherwise specified).

[2]Achieved response rates were calculated as the number of responding institutions divided by the number of sampled institutions minus those 10 schools that might well have been eliminated from the sample because of aggregate responses (schools listed separately by the U.S. Office of Education that consider themselves one unit and returned a single set of questionnaires) or closings and mergers.

Table A-1. Response rates for Carnegie Council Surveys, 1978

	Public & Private	Public	Private
Research Universities I			
Universe	51	29	22
Sample	50	28	22
Respondents	40	23	17
Research Universities II			
Universe	47	33	14
Sample	47	33	14
Respondents	37	27	10
Doctorate-granting Universities I			
Universe	56	38	18
Sample	56	38	18
Respondents	44	29	15
Doctorate-granting Universities II			
Universe	30	19	11
Sample	29	19	10
Respondents	25	18	7
Comprehensive Universities and Colleges I			
Universe	375	247	128
Sample	154	70	84
Respondents	116	48	68

Comprehensive Universities and Colleges II			
Universe	207	101	106
Sample	179	88	91
Respondents	112	51	61
Liberal Arts Colleges I			
Universe	123	–	123
Sample	66	–	66
Respondents	47	–	47
Liberal Arts Colleges II			
Universe	459	11	448
Sample	98	11	87
Respondents	61	9	52
Two-Year Colleges			
Universe	1134	904	228
Sample	191	120	71
Respondents	109	76	33
Total			
Universe	2481	1383	1098
Sample	870	407	463
Respondents	591	281	310

Note: The Ns for the universe are the number of institutions actually listed for each designated Carnegie classification and control type in *A Carnegie Classification of Institutions: Revised Edition* (1976) minus the number of schools not located in the 50 states or in Washington, D.C.

Two-Year Colleges stand apart as markedly more reluctant to participate in the survey, probably because the lengthy and detailed questionnaires were unsuited to their type of institution. Some of these schools are very small with limited staff resources, and others offer a specialized curriculum (for example, funeral services or dental hygiene) or mission (preparing clergy for their duties).

The different sample ratios and different response rates within the 17 control and Carnegie types made a differential weighting of institutions necessary. A series of weights was developed for each Carnegie type and control category. The "weight unadjusted for nonresponse" is the reciprocal of the sampling ratio; the "weight adjusted for nonresponse" is the reciprocal of the ratio of respondents to the "revised universe" within the appropriate sampling stratum.

The universe of 2,481 institutions, our sample of 870 institutions, and the 591 respondents to our survey were compared for possible sampling or response bias. These three-way comparisions concerned control, regional distribution by control, enrollment size by control, and relative changes in enrollment (between 1969 and 1977) by control. In addition, the responding institutions and the full sample were compared along the dimensions of selectivity and age. The resulting tabulations satisfied us that our sample and respondents adequately represent American higher education.[3]

Soon after the first tabulations of the written responses were available, members of the Council's staff visited 28 institutions across the country to obtain a first-hand impression of the ways in which campuses were adapting to current trends and circumstances. These visits also provided an opportunity to clarify ambiguous responses to items in the questionnaires and to obtain more detailed information about certain programs and practices that came to our attention through the surveys. On each campus, Carnegie staff members visited with

[3]Greater detail about these comparative tabulations will be available in a technical report being prepared for the custody of The Carnegie Foundation for the Advancement of Teaching.

the president, the official who had responded to the questionnaire for vice presidents or planning officers, and a group of
5 to 10 students. Many of the findings from these site visits
are presented in this and related reports of the Council.

Copies of the questionnaires used in the Carnegie Council's
1978 survey may be obtained from The Carnegie Foundation
for the Advancement of Teaching, which also retains the master
tapes on the survey.

References

American Council on Education (ACE). *A Fact Book on Higher Education.* Second issue. Washington, D.C.: 1977.

Astin, A. W., King, M. R., and Richardson, G. T. *The American Freshman: National Norms for Fall 1978.* Washington, D.C.: American Council on Education, Cooperative Institutional Research Program, 1978.

Astin, A. W., and Lee, C. B. T., *The Invisible Colleges: A Profile of Small, Private Colleges with Limited Resources.* New York: McGraw-Hill, 1972.

Baldridge, J. V., Curtis, D., Ecker, G., and Riley, G. *Policy Making and Effective Leadership: A National Study of Academic Management.* San Francisco: Jossey-Bass, 1978.

Bayer, A. *Teaching Faculty in Academe; 1972-73.* Washington, D.C.: American Council on Education, 1973.

Berg, I. *Education and Jobs: The Great Training Robbery.* New York: Praeger, 1970.

Bird, C. *The Case Against College.* New York: McKay, 1975.

Carnegie Commission on Higher Education. *Quality and Equality: New Levels of Federal Responsibility for Higher Education.* New York: McGraw-Hill, 1968.

Carnegie Commission on Higher Education. *The Open-Door Colleges: Policies for Community Colleges.* New York: McGraw-Hill, 1970.

Carnegie Commission on Higher Education. *From Isolation to Mainstream: Problems of the Colleges Founded for Negroes.* New York: McGraw-Hill, 1971.

Carnegie Commission on Higher Education. *The Fourth Revolution: Instructional Technology in Higher Education.* New York: McGraw-Hill, 1972.

Carnegie Commission on Higher Education. *College Graduates and Jobs: Adjusting to a New Labor Market Situation.* New York: McGraw-Hill, 1973a.

Carnegie Commission on Higher Education. *Governance of Higher Education: Six Priority Problems.* New York: McGraw-Hill, 1973b.

Carnegie Commission on Higher Education. *Opportunities for Women in Higher Education: Their Current Participation, Prospects for the Future, and Recommendations for Action.* New York: McGraw-Hill, 1973c.

Carnegie Commission on Higher Education. *Priorities for Action: Final Report of the Carnegie Commission on Higher Education.* New York: McGraw-Hill, 1973d.

Carnegie Council on Policy Studies in Higher Education. *Making Affirmative Action Work in Higher Education: An Analysis of Institutional and Federal Policies with Recommendations.* San Francisco: Jossey-Bass, 1975a.

Carnegie Council on Policy Studies in Higher Education. *The Federal Role in Postsecondary Education: Unfinished Business, 1975-1980.* San Francisco: Jossey-Bass, 1975b.

Carnegie Council on Policy Studies in Higher Education. *A Classification of Institutions of Higher Education: Revised Edition.* Berkeley, Calif.: Carnegie Council on Policy Studies in Higher Education, 1976.

Carnegie Council on Policy Studies in Higher Education. *Fair Practices in Higher Education: Rights and Responsibilities of Students and Their Colleges in a Period of Intensified Competition for Enrollments.* San Francisco: Jossey-Bass, 1979a.

Carnegie Council on Policy Studies in Higher Education. *Next Steps for the 1980s in Student Financial Aid: A Fourth Alternative.* San Francisco: Jossey-Bass, 1979b.

Carnegie Council on Policy Studies in Higher Education. *Three Thousand Futures: The Next Twenty Years for Higher Education.* San Francisco: Jossey-Bass, 1980.

The Carnegie Foundation for the Advancement of Teaching. *The States and Higher Education: A Proud Past and a Vital Future.* San Francisco: Jossey-Bass, 1976.

The Carnegie Foundation for the Advancement of Teaching. *Missions of the College Curriculum: A Contemporary Review with Suggestions.* San Francisco: Jossey-Bass, 1977.

Cartter, A. M. *Ph.D.'s and the Academic Labor Market.* New York: McGraw-Hill, 1976.

Cohen, A. M., and Brawer, F. B. *The Two-Year College Instructor Today.* New York: Praeger Special Studies, 1977.

Corson, J. J. "Trusteeship, 1977 Style." *AGB Reports,* Jan.-Feb. 1977, *19,* 3-5.

"Cost of Living Outpaces Year's Rise in Faculty Pay." *Chronicle of Higher Education,* March 12, 1979, p. 12.

Creager, J. A., Astin, A. W., Boruch, R. F., Bayer, A. E., and Drew, D. E. *National Norms for Entering College Freshmen—Fall 1969.* Washington, D.C.: American Council on Education, 1969.

Fadil, V. and Thrift, J. S. *Openings, Closings, Mergers, and Accreditations: Status of Independent Colleges and Universities.* National Association of Independent Colleges and Universities, 1978.

Fernandez, L. *U.S. Faculty After the Boom: Demographic Projections to 2000.* Berkeley, Calif.: Carnegie Council on Policy Studies in Higher Education, 1978.

Garbarino, J. W. *Faculty Bargaining: Change and Conflict.* New York: McGraw-Hill, 1975.

Garbarino, J. W. "State Experience in Collective Bargaining." In Carnegie Council on Policy Studies in Higher Education, *Faculty Bargaining in Public Higher Education.* San Francisco: Jossey-Bass, 1977.

Glenny, L. A., Shea, J. R., Ruyle, J. H., and Freschi, K. H. *Presidents Confront Reality: From Edifice Complex to University Without Walls.* San Francisco: Jossey-Bass, 1976.

Gross, E., and Grambsch, P. V. *Changes in University Organization, 1964-1971.* New York: McGraw-Hill, 1974.

Henry, D. D. *Challenges Past, Challenges Present: An Analysis of American Higher Education Since 1930.* San Francisco: Jossey-Bass, 1975.

Hodgkinson, H. L. *Institutions in Transition: A Profile of Change in Higher Education.* New York: McGraw-Hill, 1971.

Jencks, C., and Riesman, D. *The Academic Revolution.* New York: Doubleday, 1968.

Ladd, E. C., Jr., and Lipset, S. M. *The Character and Opinions of the American Professoriate: The Chronicle of Higher Education Special Series, 1975-76.* Storrs, Conn.: Social Science Data Center, University of Connecticut (reprinted from *Chronicle of Higher Education*), 1976.

Lauter, P. "The Exploitation of Part-Time Professors." *Chronicle of Higher Education,* May 14, 1979, p. 72.

Levine, A. *Handbook on Undergraduate Curriculum.* San Francisco: Jossey-Bass, 1978.

Levine, A. *When Dreams and Heroes Died: Portrait of Today's College Student.* San Francisco: Jossey-Bass, forthcoming.

Magarell, J. "Who Controls the Universities?" *Chronicle of Higher Education,* Sept. 6, 1977, p. 8.

Magarell, J. "Enrollments Up a Surprising 2.4 Pct." *Chronicle of Higher Education,* Nov. 5, 1979, p. 6.

"More Collegians Living on Their Own." *San Francisco Chronicle,* Dec. 28, 1979.

National Center for Education Statistics. *Fall Enrollments in Higher Education, Preliminary Survey, 1970.* Washington, D.C.: Government Printing Office, 1970.

National Center for Education Statistics. *Digest of Education Statistics, 1971.* Washington, D.C.: Government Printing Office, 1972.

National Center for Education Statistics. *Digest of Education Statistics 1977-78.* Washington, D.C.: Government Printing Office, 1978a.

National Center for Education Statistics. *Fall Enrollments in Higher Education, Preliminary, 1978, Unpublished Data.* Washington, D.C.: Government Printing Office, 1978b.

National Center for Education Statistics. *Projections of Education Statistics to 1986-87.* Washington, D.C.: Government Printing Office, 1978c.

National Center for Education Statistics. *The Condition of Education, 1978 Edition.* Washington, D.C.: Government Printing Office, 1978d.

National Center for Education Statistics. *Digest of Education Statistics, 1979.* Washington, D.C.: Government Printing Office, 1979.

National Center for Education Statistics. *Education Directory, Colleges and Universities.* Washington, D.C.: Government Printing Office, Editions for 1975, 1976, 1977, 1978, 1979.

O'Toole, J. "Tenure: A Conscientious Objection." *Change,* June-July 1978, pp. 24-31.

Paltridge, J. G., Hurst, J., and Morgan, A. *Boards of Trustees: Their Decision Patterns.* Berkeley: Center of Research and Development in Higher Education, University of California, 1973.

"Percentage of Faculty Members with Tenure, 1978-79." *Chronicle of Higher Education,* May 14, 1979, p. 14.

Perkins, J. A. "Conflicting Responsibilities of Governing Boards." In J. A. Perkins (Ed.), *The University as an Organization.* New York: McGraw-Hill, 1973.

Riesman, D., and Stadtman, V. A. *Academic Transformation: Seventeen Institutions Under Pressure.* New York: McGraw-Hill, 1973.

Thompson, D. "Democracy and the Governing of the University." *Annals of the American Academy of Political and Social Sciences,* Nov. 1972.

Trow, M. *Teachers and Students: Aspects of American Higher Education.* New York: McGraw-Hill, 1975.

U.S. Bureau of the Census. "School Enrollment: October 1969." *Current Population Reports.* Series P-20, No. 206. Washington, D.C.: Government Printing Office, 1970.

U.S. Bureau of the Census. *Statistical Abstract of the United States 1978.* Washington, D.C.: Government Printing Office, 1978.

U.S. Bureau of the Census. "School Enrollment—Social and Economic Characteristics of Students: October 1977." *Current Population Reports.* Series P-20, No. 333. Washington, D.C.: Government Printing Office, 1979.

Webster College. *Webster College: A Self-Study Report.* St. Louis, Mo.: Sept. 1977 (mimeo.).

Index